The Numbers & The Words:

ENGLISH QABALLA AND THE
BOOK OF THE LAW

ISBN 978-1-914166-20-4 (Hardcover)
ISBN 978-1-914166-21-1 (Paperback)

A catalogue for this title is available from the British Library.
10 9 8 7 6 5 4 3 2 1

First published in 2022 by Hadean Press
West Yorkshire
England

The Numbers & The Words:

ENGLISH QABALLA AND THE
BOOK OF THE LAW

Cath Thompson

for Jim

Contents

Explanatory Note

The purposed application of numbers to language first appears in the historical record in 8th century BCE Assyrian architecture, with structural measurements devised for their numeric symbolism. The development of written alphabets led to more sophisticated ideas about enumerative techniques in both Greek and Hebrew: isopsephy and gematria are closely related in their beginnings. Insofar as words are the currency of thought, converting them into numbers allows interpretation of their meaning according to numeric and literal associations, and mathematical laws. This exercise refines the intellectual ability to function beyond the merely rational and familiar sequences of ego-mentality, and to use symbols rather than words, organising the structure of the conscious mind with patterns integrated through numbers in the primary alphabetical language already understood by the intellect. The Hebrew alphabet and the pattern of the Sepher Sephiroth became the gematria of the Magickal Revival, notwithstanding the problems of aligning modern scientific discoveries with the twenty-two letters. However sublime the refinements of Hebrew Kabbalah though, the alphabet does not adequately translate into the 26 English letters, of which the *Book of the Law* is almost entirely composed. A supposed holy book requires proving by its own gematria in its own language and although the *Book of the Law* hinted at an alternative magical alphabet for the New Aeon, this was not obtained until 1976 when James Lees discovered the "order & value of the English Alphabet" and called it English Qaballa.

English Qaballa is the numeric Key to *Liber AL*, indicated within the text. It has opened the *Book of the Law* not just as a narrative in three consecutive parts, but also as a collection of numerical sets of multiple words, phrases, and sentences of particular significance and meaning that may be studied together or in isolation. The controversies which surround the manuscript are of no relevance to EQ, for it is not bound to *Liber AL* alone but applies to the whole English language.

Lees and the first generation of E. Qaballists naturally started with the vocabulary of *Liber AL*, and expanded the enumerated lexicon for practical purposes with English words used in other magical traditions. Repeated references to "the stars" for example encouraged the inclusion of the Zodiacal and planetary names for enumeration, analysis, and experiment. These operations proved the virtue of the Qaballa in revealing the magical power inherent in the English language. Correspondences with the Hebrew system demonstrated that EQ addresses the same original mystery persisting in the same conscious imagery even in modern English.

In the half-century since its discovery, English Qaballa has been used in the conjuration of spirits and the drawing of sigils, in meditation and dream interpretation, for the composition of liturgy and invocation, in exorcisms and in divination. It has also revealed an alternative magical philosophy in the structure of its correspondences, and a new ritual formula for self-initiation. English Qaballa is demonstrably a complete magical technology designed for the modern era.

This book is intended to be a useful reference for anybody who wishes to explore the possibilities of the new system. The enumeration of the text uses ( ) to indicate a phrase or clause total, [ ] to indicate a total sentence value, and { } to indicate the value of a whole verse.

The sequence of the E. Qaballistic alphabet is:

1=A, 2=L, 3=W, 4=H, 5=S, 6=D, 7=O, 8=Z, 9=K, 10=V, 11=G, 12=R, 13=C, 14=N, 15=Y, 16=J, 17=U, 18=F, 19=Q, 20=B, 21=M, 22=X, 23=I, 24=T, 25=E, 26=P.

The Enumerated Text of Liber AL

1. Had![11] The manifestation of Nuit. [356] {367}
   11   53   200   25 78

2. The unveiling of the company of heaven. {471}
   53   139   25 53   97   25   79

3. Every man and every woman is a star. {348}
   87   36   21   87   46   28 1 42

4. Every number is infinite; (388) there is no
   87   109   28   164   90   28 21

   difference. (318) {706}
       179

5. Help me,(103) o warrior lord of Thebes, (232)
   57   46   7   70   27 25   103

   in my unveiling before the Children of
   37 36   139   107   53   99   25

   men! (556) {891}
     60

6. Be thou Hadit, (155) my secret centre, (253)
   45   52   58   36   104   113

   my heart & my tongue! (236) {644}
   36   66   36   98

7. Behold! (64) it is revealed by Aiwass the
     64   47 28   106   35   38   53

minister of Hoor-paar-kraat. (596) {660}
147   25   117

8. The Khabs is in the Khu, (240) not the Khu
   53   39   28 37 53   30   45   53   30

   in the Khabs. (257) {497}
   37 53   39

9. Worship then the Khabs, (239) and behold my
   80   67   53   39   21   64   36

   light shed over you! (318) {557}
   64   40   54   39

10. Let my servants be few& secret: (378) they shall
    51 36   96   45 46   104   68   14

    rule the many & the known. (342) {720}
    56   53   51   53   47

11. These are fools that men adore; (324) both their
    83   38   39   53   60   51   55   88

    Gods & their men are fools. (397) {721}
    29   88   60   38   39

12. Come forth, (131) o children, (106) under the
    66   65   7   99   74   53

    stars, (174) & take your fill of love! (224) {635}
    47   59   51 45 25 44

THE NUMBERS & THE WORDS

13. I am above you and in you. [244] My ecstasy
    23 22   63   39 21 37 39   36   88

    is in yours. [245] My joy is to see your
    28 37   56   36 38 28 31 55   51

    joy. [277] {766}
    38

14. Above, (63) the gemmèd azure is
        63   53   109   63 28

    The naked splendour of Nuit; (578)
     53   55   114   25 78

    She bends in ecstasy to kiss
    34   70   37   88   31 42

    The secret ardours of Hadit. (602) [1243]
    53   104   60   25   58

    The wingèd globe, (200) the starry blue, (186)
     53   82   65   53   69   64

    Are mine,(121) O Ankh-af-na-khonsu!(125) [632] {1875}
    38   83   7   118

15. Now ye shall know that the chosen priest &
    24 40   14   33   53 53   68   115

    apostle of infinite space is the prince-priest
       90   25   164   70 28 53   228

the Beast; (1186) and in his woman called the
53   75   21 37 32   46   49   53

Scarlet Woman is all power given. (555) [1741]
82   46 28 5   73   83

They shall gather my children into their
68   14   77   36   99   68   88

fold: (483) they shall bring the glory of the stars
33   68   14   80   53   47 25 53   47

into the hearts of men. (664) [1147] {2888}
68   53   71   25 60

16. For he is ever a sun, (203) and she a moon. (105) [308]
37 29 28 72 1 36   21 34 1   49

But to him is the winged secret flame, (474) and
61 31 48 28 53   82   104   67   21

to her the stooping starlight. (369) [843] {1151}
31 41 53   117   106

17. But ye are not so chosen. {264}
61 40 38 45 12   68

18. Burn upon their brows, (262) o splendrous
63   64   88   47   7   119

serpent! (257) {519}
131

19. O azure-lidded woman, (184) bend upon
    7   131   46   65   64

    them! (203) {387}
      74

20. The key of the rituals is in the secret word which
    53 49 25 53   84   28 37 53 104   28   47

    I have given unto him. {817}
    23 40   83   62   48

21. With the God & the Adorer I am nothing: (389)
    54 53 24   53   63 23 22   97

    they do not see me. (227) [616] They are as upon
    68 13 45 55 46   68 38 6   64

    the earth; (295) I am Heaven, (124) and there
    53   66   23 22   79   21   90

    is no other God than me, (345) and my lord
    28 21   72   24   43   46   21 36 27

    Hadit. (142) [906] {1522}
      58

22. Now, (24) therefore, (152) I am known to ye
     24   152   23 22   47   31 40

    by my name Nuit, (373) and to him by a secret
    35 36   61   78   21 31 48 35 1 104

name which I will give him when at last he
61   47 23 30   69   48   46   25 32 29

knoweth me. (782) [1331] Since I am Infinite
   86   46   80 23 22   164

Space, (359) and the Infinite Stars thereof, (400)
   70   21   53   164   47   115

do ye also thus. (118) [877] Bind nothing! [160]
13 40 15   50   63   97

Let there be no difference made among you
51   90 45 21   179   53   54   39

between any one thing & any other thing; (998)
   136   30 46   76   30   72   76

for thereby there cometh hurt. (403) [1401] {3769}
37   125   90   94   57

23. But whoso availeth in this, (270) let him be the
    61   26   90   37 56   51 48 45 53

chief of all! (310) {580}
83 25 5

24. I am Nuit, (123) and my word is six and
    23 22   78   21 36   28 28 50 21

fifty. (282) {405}
98

25. Divide, (93) add, (13) multiply, (130) and
      93   13   130   21

    understand.(145) {381}
        124

26. Then   saith   the   prophet   and   slave   of   the
      67   57   53   124   21   43   25   53

    beauteous one: [630] Who am I, (59) and what
        141   46   14 22 23   21   32

    shall be the sign? (218) [277] So she answered
      14   45 53   53   12 34   91

    him, (185) bending down, (143) a lambent flame
      48   113   30   1   107   67

    of blue, (264) all-touching, (118) all penetrant, (170)
    25 64   118   5   165

    her lovely hands upon the black earth, (360)
      41   61   30   64   53   45   66

    & her lithe body arched for love, (309) and her
        41   78   48   61   37   44   21   41

    soft feet not hurting the little flowers: (583) [2132]
    54   92   45   105   53 100   72

    Thou knowest! [139] And the sign shall be my
        52   87   21   53   53   14   45 36

ecstasy, (310) the consciousness of the continuity
  88   53   153   25 53   174

of existence,(659) [*the un(f)ragmentary / the*
25   176   53   167   53

non-atomic fact of my universality / unmolestability]
   124   56 25 36   171   223

the omnipresence of my body.(372) [1341] {4519}
53   210   25 36 48

Write this in whiter words]
  87   56 37 91   33

But go forth on]
 61 18 65 21

27. Then the priest answered & said unto the Queen
    67 53 115   91   35 62 53   100

of Space, (671) kissing her lovely brows, (239)
25 70   90   41 61   47

and the dew of her light bathing his whole body
 21 53 34 25 41 64   97   32 41   48

in a sweet-smelling perfume of sweat:(906)[1816]
37 1   185   144   25 58

O Nuit, (85) continuous one of Heaven,(291) let
7 78   141   46 25 79   51

it be ever thus; (265) that men speak not of
47 45 72 50   53 60 66 45 25

Thee as One but as None; (506) and let them
78 6 46 61 6 60   21 51 74

speak not of thee at all, (390) since thou art
66 45 25 78 25 5   80 52 37

continuous! (310) [1847] {3663}
141

28. None,[60] breathed the light,(234) faint & faery,(151)
60   117 53 64   80 71

of the stars, (125) [510] and two. [55] {625}
25 53 47   21 34

29. For I am divided for love's sake, (307) for the
37 23 22 99 37 49 40   37 53

chance of union.(260) {567}
70 25 75

30.This is the creation of the world, (364) that the
56 28 53 119 25 53 30   53 53

pain of division is as nothing, (437) and the
64 25 111 28 6 97   21 53

joy of dissolution all. (275) {1076}
38 25 133 5

31. For these fools of men and their woes care not
      37   83   39 25 60 21   88   40   51 45

    thou at all! [571] They feel little; (238) what
      52 25 5   68 70 100   32

    is, (60) is balanced by weak joys; (226) but ye
      28   28   82   35 38 43   61 40

    are my chosen ones. (294) [818] {1389}
      38 36   68   51

32. Obey my prophet! (227) follow out the ordeals
      67   36   124   39   48 53   58

    of my knowledge! (361) seek me only! (148) [736]
      25 36   102   64 46 38

    Then the joys of my love will redeem ye from
      67   53   43 25 36 44   30   114   40 58

    all pain. [579] This is so: (96) I swear it by the
      5   64   56 28 12   23   46   47 35 53

    vault of my body; (367) by my sacred heart and
      54   25 36 48   35 36   62   66   21

    tongue; (318) by all I can give, (160) by all
      98   35 5 23 28   69   35 5

    I desire of ye all. (229) [1170] {2485}
      23   96   25 40 5

THE NUMBERS & THE WORDS

33. Then the priest fell into a deep trance or
    67   53   115   47   68 1   82   89   19

   swoon, (577) & said unto the Queen of
     36   35   62   53   100 25

   Heaven; (354) [931] Write unto us the ordeals; (282)
     79   87   62 22 53   58

   write unto us the rituals; (308) write unto us
    87   62 22 53   84   87   62 22

   the law! (230) [820] {1751}
    53 6

34. But she said: [130] the ordeals I write not: (266)
    61 34 35   53   58 23 87   45

   the rituals shall be half known and half
    53   84   14 45 25   47   21   25

   concealed:(420) the Law is for all.(129)[815]{945}
     106   53   6 28 37 5

35. This that thou writest is the threefold book of
    56   53   52   116 28 53   123   43 25

   Law. {555}
    6

36. My scribe Ankh-af-na-khonsu, (252) the priest
    36   98   118   53 115

of the princes, (364) shall not in one letter
25 53   118   14   45 37 46   112

change this book;(421) but lest there be folly,(296)
 68   56   43   61 56 90 45 44

he shall comment thereupon by the wisdom of
29 14   125   154   35 53   65   25

Ra-Hoor-Khu-it. (620) {1953}
   120

37. Also the mantras and spells; (232) the obeah
   15   53   78   21   65   53   57

and the wanga; (214) the work of the wand
  21 53   30   53 31 25 53   24

and the work of the sword; (402) these he shall
  21 53 31 25 53   33   83 29 14

learn and teach. (268) {1116}
  54   21   67

38. He must teach; (163) but he may make severe
   29 67   67   61 29 37   56   102

the ordeals. (396) {559}
  53   58

39. The word of the Law is Θελημα. {193}
   53   28   25 53   6 28

40. Who calls us Thelemites will do no wrong, (348)
    14   23 22   178   30 13 21   47

    if he look but close into the word. (357) [705]
    41 29 25   61   52   68   53   28

    For there are therein Three Grades, (442) the
    37   90   38   127   90   60   53

    Hermit, (162) and the Lover, (130) and the man
       109   21 53   56   21 53 36

    of Earth. (201) [935] Do what thou wilt shall be
    25 66   13 32   52   52 14 45

    the whole of the Law. [386] {2026}
    53   41 25 53 6

41. The word of Sin is Restriction. [358] O man! (43)
    53   28   25 42 28   182   7 36

    refuse not thy wife, (259) if she will! (105) [407]
    102   45 43 69   41 34 30

    O lover, (63) if thou wilt, (145) depart! (94) [302]
    7 56   41 52   52   94

    There is no bond that can unite the divided but
      90   28 21 47   53 28 103 53   99   61

    love: (627) all else is a curse. (163) [790] Acccurséd! [92]
    44   5 57 28 1 72   92

Accurséd be it to the aeons![320] Hell.[33] {2302}
  92   45 47 31 53   52   33

42. Let it be that state of manyhood bound and
    51 47 45 53   79 25   75   64   21

    loathing. [546] So with thy all; (114) thou hast
      86   12 54 43 5   52 34

    no right but to do thy will. (359) [473] {1019}
    21   74   61 31 13 43   30

43. Do that,(66) and no other shall say nay.(179){245}
    13 53   21 21 72   14 21 30

44. For pure will,(147) unassuaged of purpose,(245)
    37 80   30   102   25 118

    delivered from the lust of result, (403) is every
     134   58   53 48 25 85   28 87

    way perfect. (277) {1072}
    19   143

45. The Perfect and the Perfect are one Perfect and
    53   143   21 53   143   38 46   143   21

    not two; (740) nay, (30) are none! (98) {868}
    45 34   30   38 60

46. Nothing is a secret key of this law. [366]
     97   28 1   104   49 25 56   6

Sixty-one the Jews call it;(302) I call it eight, (175)
135   53   49   18 47   23 18 47 87

eighty,(102) four hundred & eighteen. (289) [868] {1234}
102   54   84   151

47. But they have the half: (247) unite by thine art
61   68   40   53   25   103 35   90   37

so that all disappear. (460) {707}
12 53   5   125

48. My prophet is a fool with his one,(355) one,(46)
36   124   28 1 34   54   32 46   46

one; (46) are not they the Ox, (233) and none
46   38 45 68 53 29   21   60

by the Book? (212) {892}
35 53   43

49. Abrogate are all rituals, (228) all ordeals, (63)
101   38   5   84   5   58

all words and signs. (117) [408] Ra-Hoor-Khuit
5   33   21   58   120

hath taken his seat in the East at the Equinox of
33   73   32 55 37 53   55 25 53   127   25

the Gods; (770) and let Asar be with Isa, (219)
53   29   21 51 19 45 54 29

who also are one. (113) [1102] But they are not
14   15   38   46   61   68   38   45

of me.[283] Let Asar be the adorant,(233) Isa,(29)
25 46   51   19   45 53   65   29

the sufferer; (185) Hoor in his secret name and
53   132   30 37 32 104   61   21

splendour is the Lord initiating.(687)[1134]{2927}
   114   28 53 27   180

50. There is a word to say about the Hierophantic
    90   281   28 31 21   69   53   176

task.[536] Behold! (64) there are three ordeals
 39   64   90   38   90   58

in one, (359) and it may be given in three
37   46   21 47 37   45   83 37   90

ways. (384) [807] The gross must pass through
 24   53   40   67   37   79

fire; (354) let the fine be tried in intellect, (508)
78   51 53 80 45 90 37   152

and the lofty chosen ones in the highest.(445)[1307]
21   53   66   68   51 37 53   96

Thus ye have star & star,(214) system & system;(190)
 50 40 40 42   42   95   95

let not one know well the other!(332)[736]{3386}
51 45   46   33   32   53   72

51.There are four gates to one palace;(393) the
90   38   54   66   31   46   68   53

floor of that palace is of silver and gold; (422)
46   25 53   68   28 25 77   21   26

lapis lazuli & jasper are there; (323) and all rare
57   53   85   38   90   21   5   50

scents; (162) jasmine & rose, (154) and the
86   105   49   21   53

emblems of death. (278) [1732] Let him enter in
119   25   60   51   48   100   37

turn or at once the four gates;(579) let him stand
67   19 25 59   53   54   66   51   48   50

on the floor of the palace.(415) [994] Will he
21   53   46   25 53   68   30   29

not sink? [155] Amn. [36] Ho! (11) warrior, (70)
45   51   36   11   70

if thy servant sink? (226) [307] But there are
41 43   91   51   61   90   38

means and means.[342] Be goodly therefore:(245)
66   21   66   45   48   152

dress ye all in fine apparel; (308) eat rich
53   40 5 37 80   93   50 52

foods and drink sweet wines and wines that
43   21   64   82   70   21   70   53

foam! (573) [1126] Also, (15) take your fill and
47   15   59   51 45 21

will of love as ye will, (351) when, (46) where
30 25 44 6 40 30   46   69

and with whom ye will! (249) [661] But always
21   54   35   40 30   61   27

unto me. [196] {5549}
62   46

52. If this be not aright; (262) if ye confound
41 56 45 45   75   41 40   96

the space-marks, (348) saying: (69) [679]
53   118   69

They are one; [152] or saying, [88] They are
68   38   46   19   69   68   38

many; [157] if the ritual be not ever unto
51   41 53   79   45 45 72 62

me: (443) then expect the direful judgments of
46   67   135   53   103   139   25

Ra Hoor Khuit! (642) [1085] {2161}
13   30   77

53. This shall regenerate the world, (327) the little
    56   14   174   53   30   53 100

    world my sister,(313) my heart & my tongue,(236)
     30   36   94   36   66   36   98

    unto whom I send this kiss.(268) [1144] Also,(15)
     62   35   23 50   56   42   15

    o scribe and prophet, (250) though thou be of
    7   98   21   124   67   52   45 25

    the princes, (360) it shall not assuage thee nor
    53   118   47 14   45   65   78   33

    absolve thee. (430) [1055] But ecstasy be thine
       70   78   61   88   45   90

    and joy of earth: (434) ever To me! (149) [583]
    21   38 25   66   72   31 46

    To me! [77] {2859}
    31 46

54. Change not as much as the style of a letter;(442)
       68   45 6   55   6 53   71 25 1 112

    for behold! (101) thou, (52) o prophet, (131)
    37   64   52   7   124

shalt not behold all these mysteries hidden
36   45   64   5   83   155   78

therein. (593) {1319}
127

55. The child of thy bowels, (231) he shall behold
53   48   25 43   62   29 14   64

them. (181) {412}
74

56. Expect him not from the East, (394) nor from
135   48   45   58   53   55   33   58

the West; (201) for from no expected house
53   57   37   58   21   166   58

cometh that child. (535) [1130] Aum! [39] All
94   53   48   39   5

words are sacred and all prophets true; (371)
33   38   62   21   5   129   78

save only that they understand a little; (425)
41   38   53   68   124   1   100

solve the first half of the equation, (417) leave
49   53   82   25 25 53   130   63

the second unattacked. (320) [1533] But thou
53   70   134   61   52

hast all in the clear light, (359) and some, (79)
34 5 37 53   53   64   21   58

though not all, (117) in the dark. (118) [673] {3375}
  67   45 5   37 53   28

57. Invoke me under my stars! [291] Love is the
     88   46   74   36   47   44 28 53

   law, (131) love under will. (148) [279]   Nor let
    6   44   74   30   33   51

   the fools mistake love; (328) for there are love
    53 39   108   44   37 90 38 44

   and love. (274) [602] There is the dove, (219)
    21   44   90 28 53   48

   and there is the serpent. (323) [542] Choose ye
    21   90 28 53   131   61   40

   well! [133] He, (29) my prophet, (160) hath
    32   29   36   124   33

   chosen, (101) knowing the law of the fortress, (326)
    68   81   53 6 25 53   108

   and the great mystery of the House of
    21   53   73   117   25   53   58   25

   God. (449) [1065]   All these old letters of my
    24   5   83   15   117 25 36

Book are aright; (437) but ℵ is not the
43   38   75   61   28 45 53

Star. (229) [666] This also is secret: (203) my
42   56 15 28 104   36

prophet shall reveal it to the wise.(436)[639]{4217}
124   14   75 47 31 53 56

58. I give unimaginable joys on earth: (394)
23 69   172   43 21 66

certainty,(151) not faith,(115) while in life,(162)
151   45 70   57 37 68

upon death; (124) peace unutterable, (271)
64   60   90   181

rest,(66) ecstasy;(88) nor do I demand aught
66   88   33 13 23 73   57

in sacrifice.(369) {1740}
37   133

59. My incense is of resinous woods & gums; (398)
36   119   28 25   108   28   54

and there is no blood therein:(329) because of
21   90 28 21   42   127   106 25

my hair the trees of Eternity. (538) {1265}
36 40 53 91 25   162

60. My number is 11, (173)   as all their numbers who
    36   109   28   6   5   88   114   14

    are of us. (312) [485]   *[The shape of my star is -]*
    38 25 22   53   61   25 36   42 28

    The Five Pointed Star, (296) with a Circle in
    53   76   125   42   54   1   88   37

    the Middle, (316) & the circle is Red. (212) [824]
    53   83   53   88   28 43

    My colour is black to the blind, (316) but the
    36   58   28   45   31 53   65   61 53

    blue & gold are seen of the seeing. (492) [808]
    64   26   38   69 25 53   103

    Also I have a secret glory for them that love
    15   23   40   1   104   47   37   74   53   44

    me. [484] ¦2601¦
    46

61. But to love me is better than all things: (469) if
    61 31 44   46 28 130   43   5   81   41

    under the night-stars in the desert thou presently
    74   53   123   37 53   97   52   148

    burnest mine incense before me,(1150) invoking
    117   83   119   107   46   111

me with a pure heart, (358) and the Serpent
46   54   1   80   66   21   53   131

flame therein, (399) thou shalt come a little to
 67   127   52   36   66 1 100 31

lie in my bosom. (469) [2845] For one kiss wilt
50 37 36   60   37 46   42   52

thou then be willing to give all; (524) but whoso
 52   67 45   78   31 69 5   61   26

gives one particle of dust shall lose all in that
 74 . 46   126   25 52   14   39   5 37 53

hour. (598) [1122] Ye shall gather goods and
 40   40   14   77   36   21

store of women and spices; (474) ye shall wear
 73   25   70   21   97   40 14   41

rich jewels; (223) ye shall exceed the nations
 52   76   40 14   116   53   88

of the earth in splendour & pride; (698) but
25 53   66 37   114   92   61

always in the love of me, (293) and so shall ye
 27   37 53 44 25 46   21 12 14 40

come to my joy. (258) [1946] I charge you
 66   31 36 38   23   66   39

earnestly to come before me in a single robe,(683)
  123   31 66   107 46 37 1   80   64

and covered with a rich headdress. (315) [998]
  21   98   54 1 52   89

I love you! [106] I yearn to you! [160] Pale
23 44   39   23 67 31 39   54

or purple, (181) veiled or voluptuous,(242)
19   108   91 19   132

I who am all pleasure and purple, (306) and
23 14 22 5   113   21 108   21

drunkenness of the innermost sense, (464)
   146   25 53   145   74

desire you. (135) [1328] Put on the wings,(197)
  96   39   67 21 53 56

and arouse the coiled splendour within
 21   67   53   76   114   91

you: (461) come unto me! (174) [832] {9337}
 39   66   62 46

62. At all my meetings with you shall the priestess
   25 5 36   148   54 39   14 53   150

say - (545) and her eyes shall burn with desire
 21   21 41 70 14   63   54   96

as she stands bare and rejoicing in my secret
6 34   55   58   21   144   37 36   104

temple - (977) [1522] To me! [77] To me! (77)
 123   31 46   31 46

calling forth the flame of the hearts of all
 66   65   53   67   25   53   71   25 5

in   her love-chant. (608) [685] {2284}
37   41   100

63. Sing the rapturous love-song unto me! [416]
   53   53   121   81   62   46

Burn to me perfumes! [289] Wear to me
63 31 46   149   41 31 46

jewels! [194] Drink to me, (141) for I love
 76   64 31 46   37 23 44

you! (143) [284] I love you! [106] {1289}
 39   23 44 39

64. I am the blue-lidded daughter of Sunset; (445)
   23 22 53   132   100   25   90

I am the naked brilliance of the voluptuous
23 22 53   55   135   25 53   132

night-sky. (603) {1048}
 105

1. Nu! (31) the hiding of Hadit. (217) {248}
   31   53   81   25   58

2. Come! (66) all ye, (45) and learn the secret that
   66   5 40   21   54   53   104   53

   hath not yet been revealed. (617) [728] I, (23)
   33   45 64 84   106   23

   Hadit, (58) am the complement of Nu, (309) my
   58   22 53   178   25 31   36

   bride. (122) [512] I am not extended, (237) and
   86   23 22 45   147   21

   Khabs is the name of my House. (321)[558]{1798}
   39   28 53   61   25 36   58

3. In the sphere I am everywhere the centre,(554)
   37 53   97   23 22   156   53   113

   as she,(40) the circumference,(284) is nowhere
   6 34   53   231   28   90

   found. (180) {1058}
   62

4. Yet she shall be known & I never.{313}
   64 34   14   45   47   23   86

5. Behold! (64) the rituals of the old time are
   64   53   84   25 53 15   93   38

black. (406) [470] Let the evil ones be cast
45   51 53 60   51 45 43

away; (323) let the good ones be purged by the
20   51 53 31   51 45 97   35 53

prophet! (540) [863] Then shall this Knowledge
124   67 14 56   102

go aright. [332] {1665}
18   75

6. I am the flame that burns in every heart of
23 22 53   67   53   68   37 87   66 25

man, (537) and in the core of every star. (322) [859]
36   21 37 53 57 25 87   42

I am Life, (113) and the giver of Life, (248) yet
23 22 68   21 53 81 25 68   64

therefore is the knowledge of me the knowledge
152   28 53   102   25 46 53   102

of death. (710) [1071] {1930}
25   60

7. I am the Magician and the Exorcist. [410] I am
23 22 53   107   21 53   131   23 22

the axle of the wheel, (285) and the cube in the
53 50 25 53   59   21 53   75 37 53

circle. (327) [612] "Come unto me" [174] is a
88   66   62   46   28 1

foolish word:(123) for it is I that go.(206)[329]{1525}
66   28   37 47 28 23 53 18

8. Who worshipped Heru-pa-kraath have worshipped
14   137   136   40   137

me;(510) ill,(27) for I am the worshipper.(278){815}
46   27   37 23 22 53   143

9. Remember all ye that existence is pure joy; (581)
161   5 40 53   176   28 80 38

that all the sorrows are but as shadows; (298)
53   5   53   51   38   61   6   31

they pass & are done;(195) but there is that
68   37   38   52   61   90   28 53

which remains. (380) {1454}
47   101

10. O prophet! (131) thou hast ill will to learn this
7   124   52   34 27 30 31 54   56

writing. (394) {525}
110

11. I see thee hate the hand & the pen; (406) but
23 55 78   54   53   25   53 65   61

I am stronger. (216) {622}
23 22   110

12. Because of me in Thee which thou knewest
    106   25 46 37 78   47   52   105

    not. {541}
    45

13. for why?[59] Because thou wast the knower,(314)
    37 22   106   52 33 53   70

    and me. (67) [381] {440}
    21 46

14. Now let there be a veiling of this shrine: (483)
    24   51   90   45 1 108 25 56   83

    now let the light devour men and eat them up
    24 51 53   64   77   60 21 50 74 43

    with blindness! (685) {1168}
    54   114

15. For I am perfect,(225) being Not;(138) and my
    37 23 22   143   93   45   21 36

    number is nine by the fools; (397) but with the
    109   28 76 35 53 39   61 54 53

    just I am eight,(362) and one in eight:(191) Which
    62 23 22   87   21 46 37 87   47

is vital, (135) for I am none indeed. (241) [1689]
28 60   37 23 22   60   99

The Empress and the King are not of me; (457)
53   119   21 53   57   38 45 25 46

for there is a further secret. (372) [829] {2518}
37   90 28 1   112   104

16. I am The Empress & the Hierophant. [410] Thus
23 22   53   119   53   140   50

eleven, (151) as my bride is eleven. (257) [408] {818}
101   6 36   86 28 101

17. Hear me, (88) ye people of sighing! (267) [355]
42 46   40 111 25   91

The sorrows of pain and regret
53   51   25 64   21 109

Are left to the dead and the dying, (695)
38   69 31 53   38   21 53   69

The folk that not know me as yet. (336) [1031] {1386}
53 36   53 45   33 46 6 64

18. These are dead, (159) these fellows; (145) they
83   38   38   83   62   68

feel not. (183) [487] We are not for the poor
70   45   28 38 45 37 53   52

and   sad: (286)   the lords of the earth are our
21   12   53   32   25 53   66   38 36

kinsfolk. (390) [676] {1163}
   87

19. Is a God to live in a dog? [206] No! (21) but the
    28 1   24 31 60 37 1 24   21   61 53

   highest are of us.(295) [316] They shall rejoice,(203)
      96   38 25 22   68   14   121

   our chosen: (104) who sorroweth is not of
   36   68   14   99   28 45 25

   us. (233) [540] {1062}
   22

20. Beauty and strength, (242) leaping laughter and
      102   21   119   102   96   21

   delicious languor, (404) force and fire, (174) are
      121   64   75   21 78   38

   of us. (85) {905}
   25 22

21. We have nothing with the outcast and the unfit:(533)
    28 40   97   54 53   91   21 53 96

   let them die in their misery. (405) [938] For they
   51   74   54 37 88   101   37 68

feel not.[220] Compassion is the vice of kings:(361)
  70 45   122   28 53 71 25 62

stamp down the wretched & the weak:(363) this
  77   30   53   112   53 38   56

is the law of the strong: (294) this is our law and
28 53 6 25 53   73   56 28 36 6 21

the joy of the world.(346) [1364] Think not, (119)
53 38 25 53   30   74   45

o king, (64) upon that lie: (167) That Thou Must
7 57   64 53 50   53 52   67

Die: (226) verily thou shalt not die, (274) but
 54   87   52   36   45 54   61

live. (121) [971] Now let it be understood: (290)
 60   24 51 47 45   123

If the body of the King dissolve, (360) he shall
41 53 48 25 53 57   83   29 14

remain in pure ecstasy for ever. (453) [1103]
  96   37   80   88   37 72

Nuit![78] Hadit![58] Ra-Hoor-Khuit![120] The
 78   58   120   53

Sun, (89) Strength & Sight, (186) Light; (64)
 36   119   67   64

these are for the servants of the Star & the
 83   38 37 53   96   25 53 42   53

Snake. (534) [873] {5725}
 54

22. I am the Snake that giveth Knowledge & Delight
 23 22 53   54   53   97   102   95

and bright glory,(661) and stir the hearts of men
 21   94   47   21 64 53 71   25 60

with drunkenness. (494) [1155] To worship me
 54   146   31   80   46

take wine and strange drugs whereof I will tell
 59   65   21   92   51   94 23 30 53

my prophet,(805) & be drunk thereof!(218) [1023]
 36   124   45   58   115

They shall not harm ye at all.[235] It is a lie,(126)
 68   14   45   38   40 25 5   47 28 1 50

this folly against self.(229)[355] The exposure of
 56   44   79   50   53   139   25

innocence is a lie. [444] Be strong, (118) o
   148   28 1 50   45   73   7

man,(43) lust,(48) enjoy all things of sense and
 36   48   77 5   81 25 74   21

rapture: (400) fear not that any God shall deny
  117   56 45 53 30 24   14   60

thee for this. (453) [1062] {4274}
  78 37 56

23. I am alone:(94) there is no God where I am.(277){371}
  23 22   49   90 28 21 24   69   23 22

24. Behold! (64) these be grave mysteries; (342)
     64   83 45 59   155

for there are also of my friends who be
37   90   38   15 25 36   103   14   45

hermits. (517) [923] Now think not to find them
  114   24   74 45 31 61   74

in the forest or on the mountain; (704) but in
37 53   91 19 21 53   121   61 37

beds of purple, (287) caressed by magnificent
56 25 108   92   35   187

beasts of women with large limbs, (665) and fire
 80 25 70   54   51   71   21 78

and light in their eyes, (379) and masses of
21   64 37 88   70   21   62   25

flaming hair about them; (381) there shall ye
 90   40 69   74   90 14 40

find them. (279) [2695] Ye shall see them at
 61   74   40 14 55 74 25

rule, (264) at victorious armies, (253) at all the
 56   25   141   87   25 5 53

joy;(121) and there shall be in them a joy a million
38   21 90   14 45 37 74 1 38 1   92

times greater than this. (720) [1358] Beware lest
 98   110   43 56   86   56

any force another,(334) King against King!(193)[527]
 30 75   87   57   79   57

Love one another with burning hearts;(413) on
 44   46   87   54   111   71   21

the low men trample in the fierce lust of your
53 12   60   111   37 53 116   48 25 51

pride,(679) in the day of your wrath.(232) [1324] {6827}
 92   37 53 22 25 51   44

25. Ye are against the people,(321) O my chosen!(111){432}
 40 38   79   53   111   7 36   68

26. I am the secret Serpent coiled about to spring:(600)
 23 22 53   104   131   76   69 31 91

in my coiling there is joy. (322) [922] If I lift up
37 36   93   90 28 38   41 23 67 43

my head, (246) I and my Nuit are one. (242) [488]
36   36   23 21   36   78   38   46

If I droop down mine head, (271) and shoot forth
41 23   58   30   83   36   21   47   65

venom, (210) then is rapture of the earth, (356)
   77   67 28   117   25 53   66

and I and the earth are one. (268) [1105] {2515}
21 23 21   53   66   38   46

27. There is great danger in me; (343) for who doth
     90   28   73   69   37 46   37   14   41

not understand these runes shall make a great
45   124   83   73   14   56 1   73

miss. (615) [958] He shall fall down into the pit
54   29   14   23   30   68 53 73

called Because, (445) and there he shall perish
  49   106   21   90   29 14   95

with the dogs of Reason. (474) [919] {1877}
54   53   29   25   64

28. Now a curse upon Because and his kin! {366}
     24 1   72   64   106   21 32 46

29. May Because be accursèd for ever! {389}
     37   106   45   92   37   72

30. If Will stops and cries Why, (259) invoking
    41 30   67   21   78   22   111

    Because, (217)   then Will stops & does
       106   67   30   67   43

    nought. (284) {760}
       77

31. If Power asks why, (156) then is Power
    41   73   20   22   67   28   73

    weakness. (255) {411}
       87

32. Also reason is a lie; (158) for there is a factor
    15   64   28 1 50   37   90 28 1 75

    infinite & unknown; (473) & all their words
      164   78   5   88   33

    are skew-wise. (262) {893}
    38   98

33. Enough of Because! [209] Be he damned for
       78   25   106   45 29   73   37

    a dog! [209] {418}
    1   24

34. But ye, (101)   o my people, (154)   rise up &
    61   40   7 36   111   65   43

awake! (147) {402}
  39

35. Let the rituals be rightly performed with joy
  51   53   84   45   91   152   54   38

  &   beauty! {670}
      102

36. There are rituals of the elements and feasts of
  90   38   84   25 53   141   21   78   25

  the times. {706}
  53   98

37. A feast for the first night of the Prophet and his
  1   73   37 53   82   76   25 53   124   21 32

  Bride! {663}
    86

38. A feast for the three days of the writing of the
  1   73   37 53   90   27 25 53   110   25 53

  Book of the Law. {674}
    43   25 53   6

39. A feast for Tahuti and the child of the
  1   73   37   93   21   53   48   25   53

  Prophet - (528) secret, (104) O Prophet! (131) {763}
    124   104   7   124

40. A feast for the Supreme Ritual, (374) and a feast
    1   73 37 53   131   79   21 1 73

    for the Equinox of the Gods. (419) {793}
    37 53   127   25 53 29

41. A feast for fire and a feast for water; (386) a feast
    1   73 37 78 21 1 73 37   65   1 73

    for life and a greater feast for death! (481) {867}
    37 68 21 1   110   73 37   60

42. A feast every day in your hearts in the joy of
    1   73   87   22 37 51   71   37 53 38 25

    my rapture! {648}
    36   117

43. A feast every night unto Nu,(330) and the
    1   73   87   76   62   31   21   53

    pleasure of uttermost delight! (466) {796}
       113   25   159   95

44. Aye!(41) feast!(73) rejoice!(121) there is no dread
    41   73   121   90 28 21   50

    hereafter.(335) [570] There is the dissolution, (304) and
    146   90 28 53   133   21

    eternal ecstasy in the kisses of Nu.(430) [734]{1304}
    103   88   37 53   72   25 31

45. There is death for the dogs. {297}
    90 28 60 37 53 29

46. Dost thou fail? [138] Art thou sorry? [140] Is fear
    42   52 44   37 52   51   28 56

    in thine heart? [277] {555}
    37 90   66

47. Where I am these are not. {280}
    69 23 22 83 38 45

48. Pity not the fallen! [248] I never knew them. [234]
    88 45 53 62   23 86   51   74

    I am not for them. [201] I console not: (141) I
    23 22 45 37 74   23 73   45   23

    hate the consoled & the consoler. (347)[488]{1171}
    54 53   79   53   85

49. I am unique & conqueror. [286] I am not of the
    23 22   115   126   23 22 45 25 53

    slaves that perish. [364] Be they damned &
    48   53   95   45 68   73

    dead! [224] Amen. [61] (This is of the 4: (162)
    38   61   56 28 25 53

    there is a fifth who is invisible, (393) & therein
    90 28 1 87 14 28 145   127

am I as a babe in an egg.(344) [899]   ) {1834}
22 23 6 1   66   37 15 47

50. Blue am I and gold in the light of my bride: (457)
    64   22 23 21   26   37 53   64   25 36   86

    but the red gleam is in my eyes;(388) & my spangles
    61   53   43   60   28 37 36   70   36   89

    are purple & green. (358) {1203}
    38   108   87

51. Purple beyond purple:(303) it is the light higher
    108   87   108   47 28 53   64   79

    than eyesight. (446) {749}
    43   132

52. There is a veil: (179) that veil is black. (186) [365]
    90   28 1 60   53   60 28   45

    It is the veil of the modest woman; (400) it is the
    47 28 53   60 25 53   88   46   47 28 53

    veil of sorrow, (259) & the pall of death: (169)
    60 25   46   53   31 25   60

    this is none of me. (215) [1043] Tear down that
    56 28   60   25 46   62   30   53

    lying spectre of the centuries: (576) veil not
    65   130   25   53   158   60 45

your vices in virtuous words: (417) these vices
  51   76 37   115   33   83   76

are my service; (346) ye do well, (85) & I will
  38 36   113   40 13 32   23 30

reward you here and hereafter. (384) [1808] {3216}
   59   39   66   21   146

53. Fear not,(101) o prophet,(131) when these words
    56   45   7   124   46   83   33

are said, (235) thou shalt not be sorry. (229) [696]
  38 35   52   36   45 45 51

Thou art emphatically my chosen; (350) and
  52   37   157   36   68   21

blessed are the eyes that thou shalt look upon
   88   38 53   70   53   52   36   25   64

with gladness.(623) [973] But I will hide thee
  54   69   61 23 30 58   78

in a mask of sorrow: (395) they that see thee
37 1   36 25   46   68   53   55   78

shall fear thou art fallen:(475) but I lift thee
  14   56   52   37   62   61 23 67   78

up. (272) [1142] {2811}
43

54. Nor shall they who cry aloud their folly that thou
    33   14   68   14   40   33   88   44   53   52

    meanest nought avail; (668) thou shall reveal
      115   77   37   52   14   75

    it: (188) thou availest: (143) they are the slaves
    47   52   91   68   38   53   48

    of because:(338) They are not of me.(222) [1559]
    25   106   68 38 45 25 46

    The stops as thou wilt;(230) the letters? (170)
    53   67   6   52   52   53   117

    change them not in style or value!(369)[769]{2328}
    68   74   45 37 71 19 55

55.Thou shalt obtain the order & value of the
   52   36   89   53   62   55   25   53

    English Alphabet; (612) thou shalt find new
      84   103   52   36   61   42

    symbols to attribute them unto. (603) {1215}
      75   31   170   74   62

56. Begone! (102) ye mockers; (132) even though
    102   40   92   74   67

    ye laugh in my honour ye shall laugh not
    40   35   37 36   61   40   14   35   45

long: (518) then when ye are sad know that I
34   67   46   40 38   12   33   53 23

have forsaken you. (482) {1234}
40   91   39

57. He that is righteous shall be righteous still; (481)
29 53 28   128   14 45   128   56

he that is filthy shall be filthy still. (397) {878}
29 53 28 86   14 45 86   56

58. Yea! (41) deem not of change: (215) ye shall be
41   77   45 25   68   40 14 45

as ye are,(183) & not other.(117) [556] Therefore
6 40 38   45   72   152

the kings of the earth shall be Kings for ever: (641)
53   62 25 53   66   14 45 62   37 72

the slaves shall serve. (192) [833] There is none
53   48   14   77   90 28 60

that shall be cast down or lifted up: (523) all is
53   14 45 43   30   19 98   43   5 28

ever as it was. (167) [690] Yet there are masked
72 6 47 9   64 90   38   67

ones my servants: (442) it may be that yonder
51   36   96   47 37 45 53   79

beggar is a King. (427) [869] A King may choose
80   28 1   57   1   57   37   61

his garment as he will: (361)   there is no
32   108   6   29 30   90   28 21

certain test:(329) but a beggar cannot hide his
112   78   61 1   80   73   58 32

poverty. (424) [1114] {4062}
119

59. Beware therefore![238] Love all,(49) lest perchance
86   152   44 5   56   133

is a King concealed! (381) [430] Say you so? [72]
28 1 57   106   21 39 12

Fool! [34] If he be a King, (173) thou canst not
34   41 29 45 1 57   52   57   45

hurt him. (259) [432] {1206}
57   48

60. Therefore strike hard & low, (285) and to hell
152   98   23   12   21 31 33

with them, (213) master! (88) {586}
54   74   88

61. There is a light before thine eyes, (450)   o
90   28 1   64   107   90   70   7

prophet, (131)   a   light   undesired, (198)   most
124   1   64   133   57

desirable. (176) {955}
119

62. I am uplifted in thine heart; (379)   and the kisses
23 22   141   37   90   66   21   53   72

of the stars rain hard upon thy body. (499) {878}
25 53   47   50   23   64   43   48

63. Thou art exhaust in the voluptuous fullness of
52   37   98   37 53   132   88   25

the inspiration; (747)   the expiration is sweeter
53   172   53   177   28   119

than death, (480)   more rapid and laughterful
43   60   65   68   21   133

than a caress of Hell's own worm. (522) {1749}
43   1   61   25   38   24   43

64. Oh! (11)   thou art overcome: (209)   we are upon
11   52   37   120   28   38   64

thee; (208)   our   delight is   all   over thee: (296)
78   36   95   28   5   54   78

hail! (30) hail: (30)   prophet of Nu! (180)   prophet
30   30   124   25 31   124

of Had!(160) prophet of Ra-Hoor-Khu!(222)[1346]
25 11   124 25   73

Now rejoice! (145) now come in our splendour
  24   121   24   66 37 36   114

& rapture! (394) [539] Come in our passionate
   117   66 37 36   131

peace, (360) & write sweet words for the
  90   87   82   33   37 53

Kings! (354) [714] {2599}
  62

65. I am the Master: (186) thou art the Holy Chosen
  23 22 53   88   52 37 53 28   68

  One. (284) {470}
  46

66. Write, (87) & find ecstasy in writing! (296) [383]
    87   61   88 37 110

  Work, (31) & be our bed in working! (248) [279]
    31   45 36 51 37   79

  Thrill with the joy of life & death! [365] Ah! (5)
    67   54   53 38 25 68   60   5

  thy death shall be lovely: (223) whoso seeth it
    43   60   14 45 61   26   83 47

shall be glad. (235) [463] Thy death shall be the
  14   45   20   43   60   14 45 53

seal of the promise of our agelong love. [621]
  33 25 53   119   25 36   71   44

Come!(66) lift up thine heart & rejoice!(387) [453]
  66   67 43 90   66   121

We are one; (112) we are none. (126) [238] {2802}
  28 38   46   28 38   60

67. Hold![19] Hold![19] Bear up in thy rapture;(298)
    19   19   58 43 37 43   117

    fall not in swoon of the excellent kisses! (443)[741] {779}
    23 45 37   36 25 53   152   72

68. Harder![60] Hold up thyself![155] Lift thine head!(193)
    60   19 43   93   67   90   36

    breathe not so deep -(250) die!(54) [497] {712}
    111   45 12 82   54

69. Ah![5] Ah![5] What do I feel?[138] Is the word
    5   5   32   13 23 70   28 53   28

    exhausted?[238] {386}
    129

70. There is help & hope in other spells.[411] Wisdom
    90 28 57   62 37 72   65   65

says: [91] be strong! [118] Then canst thou bear
26   45 73   67 57 52 58

more joy. [337] Be not animal; (152) refine thy
65 38   45 45 62   117 43

rapture! (277) [429] If thou drink, (157) drink
117   41 52 64   64

by the eight and ninety rules of art:(498) if thou
35 53 87 21 115 61 25 37   41 52

love, (137) exceed by delicacy; (249) and if thou
44   116 35 98   21 41 52

do aught joyous, (251) let there be subtlety
13 57   67   51 90 45 132

therein! (445) [1737] {3123}
127

71. But exceed! (177) exceed! (116) {293}
61 116   116

72. Strive ever to more! (267) and if thou art truly
99 72 31 65   21 41 52 37 70

mine - (304) and doubt it not, (187) an if thou art
83   21 74 47 45   15 41 52 37

ever joyous!(284) - death is the crown of all.(220){1262}
72 67   60 28 53 49 25 5

73. Ah![5] Ah![5] Death![60] Death!(60) thou shalt
    5   5   60   60   52   36

    long for death.(219)[279] Death is forbidden,(219)
     34 37   60   60   28   131

    o man,(43) unto thee. (140) [402] {751}
    7 36   62   78

74. The length of thy longing shall be the strength
    53   80   25 43   82   14 45 53   119

    of its glory. [638] He that lives long & desires
    25 52 47   29   53   65   34   101

    death much is ever the King among the
     60   55   28 72   53   57   54   53

    Kings. [776] {1414}
      62

75. Aye!(41) listen to the numbers & the words:(377) {418}
    41   93 31 53   114   53   33

76. 4 6 3 8 A B K 2 4 A L G M O R 3 Y X
             1 20 9   1 2 11 21 7 12 15 22

    24 89 R P S T O V A L. [208] What meaneth
          12 26 5 24 7 10 1 2   32   114

    this, (202) o prophet? (131) [333] Thou knowest
    56   7   124   52   87

not; (184) nor shalt thou know ever. (226) [410]
45   33   36   52   33   72

There cometh one to follow thee: (378) he shall
90   94   46 31   39   78   29 14

expound it. (207) [585] But remember, (222) o
117   47   61   161   7

chosen one, (121) to be me; (122) to follow the
68   46   31 45 46   31   39   53

love of Nu in the star-lit heaven; (483) to look
44   25 31 37 53   91   79   31 25

forth upon men, (245) to tell them this glad
65   64   60   31 53 74   56   20

word. (262) [1455] {2991}
28

77. O be thou proud and mighty among men! {405}
7 45 52   68   21   98   54   60

78. Lift up thyself! (203) for there is none like unto
67 43   93   37   90 28 60 59   62

thee among men or among Gods!(630) [833] Lift
78   54   60 19   54   29   67

up thyself, (203) o my prophet, (167) thy stature
43   93   7 36   124   43   108

shall surpass the stars. (336) [706]   They shall
 14   71   53   47   68   14

worship   thy   name, (266)   foursquare, (133)
  80   43   61   133

mystic, (101) wonderful, (104) the number of
  101   104   53   109   25

the man; (276) and the name of thy house
 53   36   21   53   61   25 43   58

418. (261) [1141] {2680}

79. The end of the hiding of Hadit; (340)   and
    53   45   25 53   81   25   58   21

   blessing & worship to the prophet of the
     105   80   31   53   124   25 53

   lovely Star! (595) {935}
    61   42

1. Abrahadabra; (79) the reward of Ra Hoor
        79   53   59   25 13   30

   Khut. (234) {313}
   54

2.There is division hither homeward; (400) there
     90   28   111   92   79   90

   is a word not known. (239) [639]   Spelling is
   28 1 28   45   47   108   28

   defunct; (253) all is not aught. (135) [388]
     117   5 28 45   57

   Beware! [86] Hold! [19] Raise the spell of
     86   19   66   53   60   25

   Ra-Hoor-Khuit! [324] {1456}
        120

3. Now let it be first understood that I am a god
     24 51 47 45 82   123   53 23 22 1 24

   of War and of Vengeance. [720] I shall deal hardly
   25 16 21 25   138   23 14   34   40

   with them. [239] {959}
   54   74

4. Choose ye an island! {167}
     61   40 15   51

THE NUMBERS & THE WORDS

5. Fortify it! {164}
   117 47

6. Dung it about with enginery of war! {398}
   48 47 69   54   139   25 16

7. I will give you a war-engine. {290}
   23 30 69 39 1   128

8. With it ye shall smite the peoples; (422) and none
   54 47 40 14   98   53   116   21   60

   shall stand before you. (291) {713}
   14   50   107   39

9. Lurk! [40] Withdraw! [76] Upon them! (138) this is
   40   76   64   74   56 28

   the Law of the Battle of Conquest: (466) thus shall my
   53   6 25 53 96   25   124   50   14   36

   worship be about my secret house. (492) [1096] {1212}
   80   45   69   36   104   58

10. Get the stélé of revealing itself; (439) set it in thy
    60 53 81 25   123   97   54 47 37 43

    secret temple - (408) and that temple is already
    104   123   21   53   123   28   62

    aright disposed - (465) & it shall be your Kiblah
    75   103   47 14   45   51   59

for ever. (325) [1637] It shall not fade, (156)
37   72   47   14   45   50

but miraculous colour shall come back to it
61   118   58   14   66   43   31 47

day after day. (562) [718] Close it in locked glass
22   80   22   52   47 37   62   24

for a proof to the world. [444] {2799}
37 1   70 31 53   30

11.This shall be your only proof. [274] I forbid
   56   14   45   51   38   70   23   86

argument.[234] Conquer! [107] That is enough. [159]
    125   107   53 28   78

I will make easy to you the abstruction from the
23 30   56   46   31 39   53   160   58   53

ill-ordered house in the Victorious City. [1033]
   120   58   37 53   141   75

Thou shalt thyself convey it with worship, (446)
52   36   93   84 47 54   80

o prophet, (131) though thou likest it not. (299) [876]
7   124   67   52   88   47 45

Thou shalt have danger & trouble.[304] Ra-Hoor-Khu
52   36   40   69   107   73

THE NUMBERS & THE WORDS

is with thee. [233] Worship me with fire &
28 54   78   80   46 54 78

blood; (300) worship me with swords & with
  42   80   46 54   38   54

spears. (346) [646] Let the woman be girt with
  74   51 53 46 45 70 54

a sword before me: (506) let blood flow to my
1   33   107   46   51   42   30 31 36

name. (251) [757] Trample down the Heathen; (291)
  61   111   30 53   97

be upon them, (183) o warrior, (77) I will give you
45 64 74   7   70   23 30 69 39

of their flesh to eat! (409) [960] {5583}
25 88   54 31 50

12. Sacrifice cattle, (222) little and big: (175) after a
      133   89   100 21 54   80 1

    child. (129) {526}
      48

13. But not now. {130}
    61 45 24

14. Ye shall see that hour, (202) o blessèd Beast, (170) and
    40 14 55 53 40   7   88   75   21

thou the Scarlet Concubine of his desire! (507) {879}
52   53   82   146   25 32   96

15. Ye shall be sad thereof. {226}
40   14   45 12   115

16. Deem not too eagerly to catch the promises; (514)
77   45 38   91   31 55   53   124

fear not to undergo the curses. (354) [868] Ye, (40)
56   45 31   92   53   77   40

even ye,(114) know not this meaning all.(248) [402] {1270}
74 40   33 45 56   109   5

17. Fear not at all; (131) fear neither men, (243) nor
56   45 25 5   56   127   60   33

Fates   nor   gods, (168)   nor   anything. (139) [681]
73   33   29   33   106

Money   fear   not, (183)   nor   laughter   of the folk
82   56   45   33   96   25 53   36

folly, (287)   nor any other power in heaven or upon
44   33 30   72   73 37   79   19   64

the earth or under the earth.(738) [1208] Nu is your
53   66   19   74   53   66   31 28   51

refuge as Hadit your light; (397)   and I am the
108   6   58   51   64   21   23 22   53

strength, (238)   force, (75)   vigour, (80)   of your
  119   75   80   25 51

arms. (115) [905] {2794}
  39

18. Mercy let be off:(225)   damn them who pity! (218) [443]
   86   51 45 43   42   74   14   88

Kill and torture; (178)   spare not; (114)   be upon
  36   21   121   69   45   45 64

them! (183) [475] {918}
  74

19. That stélé they shall call the Abomination of
  53   81   68   14   18   53   155   25

Desolation; (581)   count well its name, (220)   & it
   114   75   32 52 61   47

shall be to you as 718. (182) {983}
  14 45 31 39 6

20. Why?[22]   Because of the fall of Because,(338)   that
  22   106   25 53 23 25   106   53

he is not there again. (295) [633] {655}
 29 28 45   90   50

21. Set up my image in the East:(359)   thou shalt buy thee
  54 43 36   81 37 53 55   52   36   52 78

an image which I will show thee,(511) especial,(120)
15   81   47   23 30   19   78   120

not unlike the one thou knowest. (373) [1363] And
45   90   53 46   52   87   21

it shall be suddenly easy for thee to do this. [478] {1841}
47 14 45   90   46 37   78 31 13 56

22. The other images group around me to support
53   72   86   73   57   46 31   117

me: (581) let all be worshipped, (238) for they shall
46   51 5 45   137   37 68   14

cluster to exalt me.(368) [1187] I am the visible
98   31   74   46   23 22 53   108

object of worship; (416) the others are secret; (272)
105   25   80   53   77   38   104

for the Beast & his Bride are they:(389) and for the
37 53   75   32   86   38 68   21 37   53

winners of the Ordeal X. (360) [1437] What is this? [116]
96   25 53   53   22   32   28 56

Thou shalt know. [121] {2861}
52   36   33

23. For perfume mix meal & honey & thick leavings of
37   144   66   49   65   73   91   25

red wine: (658)   then oil of Abramelin and olive
 43   65   67   32 25   119   21   67

oil, (363)   and afterward soften & smooth down
 32   21   102   93   68   30

with rich fresh blood. (526) {1547}
 54   52   64   42

24. The best blood is of the moon, (324)   monthly: (87)
  53   74   42 28 25 53   49   87

then the fresh blood of a child,(300)   or dropping
 67   53   64   42   25 1   48   19   125

from the host of heaven:(399) then of enemies;(230)
 58   53   40   25   79   67 25   138

then of the priest or of the worshippers: (505) last
 67   25 53   115   19 25 53   148   32

of some beast, (190) no matter what. (160) {2195}
 25   58   75   21   107   32

25. This burn:(119) of this make cakes & eat unto
   56   63   25   56   56   53   50   62

me. (348) [467] This hath also another use; (238)
 46   56   33   15   87   47

let it be laid before me, (328) and kept thick with
 51 47 45 32   107   46   21   84   73   54

perfumes of your orison: (525) it shall become full
149   25 51   68   47 14   111   39

of beetles as it were and creeping things sacred
25   126   6 47 65 21   149   81   62

unto me. (901) [1992] {2459}
62   46

26. These slay, (106) naming your enemies; (273) & they
83   23   84   51   138   68

shall fall before you. (251) {630}
14   23   107   39

27. Also these shall breed lust & power of lust in you
15   83   14   88   48   73   25 48 37 39

at the eating thereof. {761}
25 53   98   115

28. Also ye shall be strong in war. {240}
15   40   14   45   73   37 16

29. Moreover, (119) be they long kept, (231) it is
119   45 68   34   84   47 28

better; (205) for they swell with my force. (307) [862]
130   37 68   37   54 36   75

All before me. [158] {1020}
5   107   46

30. My altar is of open brass work: (275) burn thereon
    36   40 28 25 72   43   31   63   111

   in silver or gold! (333) {608}
   37 77   19 26

31. There cometh a rich man from the West who shall
    90   94   1 52   36   58   53 57   14   14

   pour his gold upon thee.{731}
   62   32   26   64   78

32. From gold forge steel! {238}
   58   26   73   81

33. Be ready to fly or to smite! {318}
   45   59   31 35 19 31   98

34. But your holy place shall be untouched throughout
    61   51   28   67   14 45   127   127

   the centuries: (731) though with fire and sword it
   53   158   67   54 78 21   33 47

   be burnt down & shattered, (588) yet an invisible
   45   87   30   126   64 15   145

   house there standeth, (475) and shall stand until
    58   90   103   21 14   50   80

   the fall of the Great Equinox;(519) when Hrumachis
   53 23 25 53   73   127   46   100

shall arise and the double-wanded one assume my
14   66   21 53   132   46   74   36

throne and place. (762) [3075] Another prophet
  86   21   67   87   124

shall arise, (291) and bring fresh fever from the
14   66   21   80   64   90   58   53

skies; (433) another woman shall awake the lust &
 67   87   46   14   39   53 48

worship of the Snake; (499) another soul of God and
  80   25 53 54   87   31 25 24 21

beast shall mingle in the globèd priest; (649) another
  75   14   96 37 53   71   115   87

sacrifice shall stain The tomb; (426) another king
 133   14   67   53   72   87   57

shall reign; (243) and blessing no longer be poured
14   85   21   105   21   71   45   93

To the Hawk-headed mystical Lord! (655) [3196] {6271}
31 53   84   104   27

35. The half of the word of Heru-ra-ha, (285) called
    53   25 25 53 28 25   76   49

Hoor-pa-kraat and Ra-Hoor-Khut. (271) {556}
        104   21   97

36. Then said the prophet unto the God: {418}
    67   35   53   124   62   53   24

37. I adore thee in the song - (279)
   23 51   78 37 53 37

    I am the Lord of Thebes, (253) and I
    23 22 53   27 25 103   21 23

    The inspired forth-speaker of Mentu; (525)
     53   134   168   25 101

    For me unveils the veilèd sky, (352)
    37 46   96   53   91   29

    The self-slain Ankh-af-na-khonsu
    53   95   118

    Whose words are truth. (462) [1871] I invoke, (111)
      44   33   38   81   23   88

    I greet
    23 97

    Thy presence, (308) O Ra-Hoor-Khuit! (127) [546]
    43   145   7   120

    Unity uttermost showed! [302]
     93   159   50

I adore the might of Thy breath, (364)
23   51   53   83   25 43   86

Supreme and terrible God, (319)
   131   21   143   24

Who makest the gods and death
14   85   53   29   21   60

To tremble before Thee - (607)
31   129   107   78

I, (23) I adore thee! (152) [1465]
23   23   51   78

Appear on the throne of Ra! [289]
   91   21 53   86   25 13

Open the ways of the Khu! [257]
72   53   24   25 53   30

Lighten the ways of the Ka! [268]
   103   53   24   25 53 10

The ways of the Khabs run through
53   24   25 53   39   43   79

To stir me or still me! [578]
31 64   46 19 56   46

Aum! (39) let it fill me! (189) [228] {5804}
39   51 47 45 46

38. So that thy light is in me; (283) & its red flame is
12 53   43   64 28 37 46   52 43   67   28

as a sword in my hand to push thy order. (516) [799]
6 1   33   37 36   25 31 52   43   62

There is a secret door that I shall make to establish
90   28 1   104   32   53 23 14   56   31   109

thy way in all the quarters, (813) (these are the
43   19 37 5 53   115   83   38   53

adorations, (274) as thou hast written, (217)   )
100   6   52   34   125

as it is said: (116) [1420]
6 47 28 35

The light is mine; (228) its rays consume
53   64 28 83   52 33   102

Me: (233) I have made a secret door
46   23 40   53 1 104   32

Into the House of Ra and Tum, (553)
68   53   58   25 13 21   62

Of Khephra and of Ahathoor. (212) [1226]
25   81   21 25   60

I am thy Theban, (176) O Mentu, (108)
23 22 43   88   7   101

The prophet Ankh-af-na-Khonsu! (295) [579]
  53   124   118

By Bes-na-Maut my breast I beat; (379)
35   128   36   87 23 70

By wise Ta-Nech I weave my spell. (355) [734]
35 56   81   23 64   36   60

Show thy star-splendour, (218) O Nuit! (85) [303]
  19   43   156   7   78

Bid me within thine House to dwell, (403)
49 46   91   90   58 31 38

O wingèd snake of light, (232) Hadit! (58) [693]
7   82   54 25 64   58

Abide with me, (175) Ra-Hoor-Khuit! (120)[295]{6049}
  75   54 46   120

39. All this and a book to say how thou didst come
    5   56 21 1 43 31 21 14   52   64   66

    hither and a reproduction of this ink and paper
      92   21 1   186   25 56 46 21   90

for ever - (1021) for in it is the word secret & not
37 72   37 37 47 28 53   28   104   45

only in the English - (591) and thy comment upon
38 37 53   84   21 43   125   64

this the Book of the Law shall be printed beautifully
56 53   43 25 53   6   14 45   130   164

in red ink and black upon beautiful paper made by
37 43 46 21   45   64   147   90   53 35

hand; (1448) and to each man and woman that thou
25   21 31 43   36   21   46   53 52

meetest, (452) were it but to dine or to drink at
149   65 47 61 31 68 19 31 64 25

them, (485) it is the Law to give. (234) [4231] Then
74   47 28 53   6 31 69   67

they shall chance to abide in this bliss or no; (513)
68   14   70   31 75 37 56   55 19 21

it is no odds. (120) [633] Do this quickly! [167] {5031}
47 28 21   24   13 56   98

40. But the work of the comment? [348] That is easy; (127)
    61 53 31 25 53   125   53 28 46

and Hadit burning in thy heart shall make swift
21   58   111   37 43 66   14   56   73

and secure thy pen. (705) [832] {1180}
21   97   43 65

41. Establish at thy Kaaba a clerk-house: (329) all must
       109   25 43   32   1   119   5 67

be done well and with business way. (409) {738}
45 52   32 21 54   114   19

42. The ordeals thou shalt oversee thyself, (401) save
      53   58   52   36   109   93   41

only the blind ones. (248) [649] Refuse none, (162)
38   53   65   51   102   60

but thou shalt know & destroy the traitors. (437) [599]
61 52   36   33   94   53   108

I am Ra-Hoor-Khuit, (165) and I am powerful to
23 22   120   21 23 22   110   31

protect my servant. (465) [630] Success is thy
   131   36   91   83   28 43

proof: (224) argue not; (111) convert not; (150)
   70   66 45   105   45

talk not overmuch! (190) [675] Them that seek to
36 45   109   74   53 64 31

entrap thee, (402) to overthrow thee, (213) them
   102   78   31   104   78   74

attack without pity or quarter; (465) & destroy
  72   102   88 19   110   94

them utterly. (287) [1367] Swift as a trodden
  74   119   73   6 1   94

serpent turn and strike! [491] Be thou yet deadlier
  131   67   21   98   45 52 64   100

than he! [333] Drag down their souls to awful
 43   29   30   30   88   36   31   41

torment: (383) laugh at their fear: (204) spit upon
  127   35   25 88   56   78   64

them! (216) [803] {5547}
  74

43. Let the Scarlet Woman beware! [318] If pity and
    51 53   82   46   86   41 88   21

    compassion and tenderness visit her heart; (640) if
       122   21   155   85 41   66   41

    she leave my work to toy with old sweetnesses; (512)
    34 63   36   31 31 46 54 15   161

    then shall my vengeance be known. (347) [1499]
     67   14   36   138   45   47

    I will slay me her child: (211) I will alienate her
    23 30 23   46 41   48   23 30   115   41

heart: (275) I will cast her out from men: (303) as
66   23 30 43 41 48 58 60   6

a shrinking and despised harlot shall she crawl
1   115   21   121   50   14 34 31

though dusk wet streets, (669) and die cold and
67   37 52 120   21 54 28 21

an-hungered. (253) [1711] {3528}
129

44. But let her raise herself in pride! [439] Let her
61 51 41 66   91 37 92   51 41

follow me in my way! [269] Let her work the work
39   46 37 36 19   51 41 31 53 31

of wickedness! [360]   Let her kill her heart! [235]
25   128   51 41 36 41 66

Let her be loud and adulterous! [306]   Let her be
51 41 45 32 21   116   51 41 45

covered with jewels,(365) and rich garments,(186) and
98   54   76   21 52   113   21

let her be shameless before all men!(423) [974] {2583}
51 41 45   93   107 5 60

45. Then will I lift her to pinnacles of power:(480) then
67   30 23 67 41 31   123   25 73   67

will I breed from her a child mightier than all
30 23　88　　58　41 1　48　　143　　43　5

the kings of the earth. (806) [1286] I will fill her
53　62　25 53　66　　　　　　23 30　45 41

with joy: (231) with my force shall she see &
54　38　　　54　36　75　14　34　55

strike at the worship of Nu: (580) she shall achieve
98　25 53　80　25 31　　34　14　101

Hadit. (207) [1018] {2304}
58

46. I am the warrior Lord of the Forties: (387) the Eighties
23 22　53　70　27 25 53　114　　53　140

cower before me, (406) & are abased. (96) [889] I will
60　107　46　　38　58　　23 30

bring you to victory & joy: (345) I will be at your arms
80　39 31　104　38　　23 30　45 25　51　39

in battle & ye shall delight to slay. (549) [894] Success
37　96　40 14　95　31 23　　83

is your proof; (232) courage is your armour; (235) go
28 51　70　　86　28　51　70　18

on, (39) go on, (39) in my strength; (192) & ye shall
21　18 21　37 36　119　40　14

turn not back for any! (276) [1013] ¦2796¦
67   45   43   37   30

47. This book shall be translated into all tongues: (448)
   56   43   14   45   114   68   5   103

but always with the original in the writing of the
61   27   54   53   93   37 53   110   25 53

Beast; (641) for in the chance shape of the letters
   75   37 37 53   70   61   25 53   117

and their position to one another: (855) in these
21   88   129   31 46   87   37   83

are mysteries that no Beast shall divine. (577) ¦2521¦
38   155   53   21   75   14   101

Let him not seek to try: (290) but one cometh after
51   48   45   64   31 51   61   46   94   80

him, (329) whence I say not, (173) who shall discover
48   84   23 21   45   14   14   101

the Key of it all. (308) [1100] Then this line drawn
53   49   25 47   5   67   56   64   36

is a key: (301) then this circle squared in its failure
28 1   49   67   56   88   85   37 52   98

is a key also. (576) [877] And Abrahadabra. [100] It
28 1   49   15   21   79   47

shall be his child & that strangely.[348] Let him not
14   45 32   48   53   109   51   48   45

seek after this; (344) for thereby alone can he fall
64   80   56   37   125   49   28 29 23

from it. (396) [740] {5686}
58   47

48. Now this mystery of the letters is done, (472) and I
24   56   117   25 53   117   28 52   21 23

want to go on to the holier place. (380) {852}
42   31 18 21 31 53   73   67

49. I am in a secret fourfold word,(302) the blasphemy
23 22 37 1   104   87   28   53   119

against all gods of men. (370) {672}
79   5   29   25 60

50. Curse them![146] Curse them! [146] Curse them![146]{438}
72   74   72   74   72   74

51. With my Hawk's head I peck at the eyes of Jesus as
54   36   22   36 23 73 25 53 70 25 68   6

he hangs upon the cross. {714}
29   35   64   53   42

52. I flap my wings in the face of Mohammed & blind
23 47   36   56   37 53 57 25   106   65

him. {553}
48

53. With my claws I tear out the flesh of the Indian and
    54   36   24 23 62   48 53   54   25 53   81   21

the Buddhist, (692) Mongol and Din. (126) {818}
    53   105   62   21 43

54. Bahlasti! [80] Ompehda! [90] I spit on your crapulous
    80   90   23 78 21 51   100

creeds. [359] {529}
    86

55. Let Mary inviolate be torn upon wheels: (459) for
    51   49   129   45 57   64   64   37

her sake let all chaste women be utterly despised
    41 40 51 5   72   70   45 119   121

among you! (694) {1153}
    54   39

56. Also for beauty's sake and love's! {269}
    15 37   107   40   21   49

57. Despise also all cowards; (182) professional soldiers
    115   15   5   47   145   85

who dare not fight, (413) but play: (105) all fools
    14   44   45 80   61 44   5   39

despise! (159) {859}
  115

58. But the keen and the proud, (329) the royal and
    61 53   73   21 53   68   53   37   21

  the lofty; (230) ye are brothers! (187) {746}
    53 66   40 38   109

59. As brothers fight ye! {235}
    6   109   80 40

60. There is no law beyond Do what thou wilt. {381}
    90 28 21 6   87   13 32   52   52

61. There is an end of the word of the God enthroned
    90 28 15 45 25 53   28   25 53   24   131

  in Ra's seat, (627) lightening the girders of the
    37 18   55   151   53   94   25 53

  soul. (407) {1034}
    31

62. To Me do ye reverence! (291) to me come ye
    31 46 13 40   161   31 46   66   40

  through tribulation of ordeal, (507) which is
    79   167   25   53   47   28

  bliss. (130) {928}
    55

63. The fool readeth this Book of the Law, (367)   and its
    53   34   97   56   43 25 53   6   21 52

    comment; (198) & he understandeth it not. (298) {863}
        125   29   177   47 45

64. Let him come through the first ordeal, (432)   & it
    51 48   66   79   53 82   53   47

    will be to him as silver. (284) {716}
    30 45 31 48   6   77

65. Through the second, (202) gold. (26) {228}
        79   53   70   26

66. Through the third, (201)   stones of precious
        79   53   69   80   25   128

    water. (298) {499}
    65

67. Through the fourth, (214) ultimate sparks of the
        79   53   82   137   58   25 53

    intimate fire. (506) {720}
    155   78

68. Yet to all it shall seem beautiful. [384] Its enemies
    64 31 5 47 14   76   147   52   138

    who say not so, (282) are mere liars. (164) [446] {830}
    14   21 45 12   38   83   43

69. There is success. {201}
   90 28   83

70. I am the Hawk-Headed Lord of Silence & of
  23 22 53   84   27 25 107   25

   Strength; (485) my nemyss shrouds the night-blue
     119   36   85   56   53   140

   sky. (399) {884}
   29

71. Hail! (30) ye twin warriors about the pillars of the
   30   40 64   75   69   53   71 25 53

   world!(480) for your time is nigh at hand.(311) {821}
   30   37 51 93 28 52 25 25

72. I am the Lord of the Double Wand of Power; (402)
  23 22 53 27 25 53   77   24 25 73

   the wand of the Force of Coph Nia - (343) but my
   53   24   25 53 75 25 50   38   61 36

   left hand is empty, (330) for I have crushed an
   69   25   28 111   37 23 40   82   15

   Universe; (328) & nought remains. (178) {1581}
   131   77   101

73. Paste the sheets from right to left and from top to
   81   53   88   58   74 31 69 21   58   57 31

bottom: (724) then behold! (131) {855}
  103   67   64

74. There is a splendour in my name hidden and
  90 28 1   114   37 36   61   78   21

glorious, (550) as the sun of midnight is ever
  84   6 53 36 25   126   28 72

the son. (425) {975}
  53   26

75. The ending of the words is the Word Abrahadabra.[445]
  53   93   25 53   33   28 53 28   79

The Book of the Law is Written
  53   43   25 53 6 28 125

and Concealed. [460]
  21   106

Aum. [39] Ha. [5] {949}
  39   5

Do what thou wilt shall be the whole of the Law. [386]
13   32   52   52   14   45 53   41   25 53   6

The study of this Book is forbidden. [403] It is wise
53   67 25 56   43 28   131   47 28 56

to destroy this copy after the first reading. [680]
31   94   56   61   80   53 82   92

Whosoever disregards this does so at his own risk
98   106   56   43 12 25 32 24   49

and peril. [554] These are most dire. [244]
21   88   83   38   57   66

Those who discuss the contents of this Book
65   14   74   53   126   25 56   43

are to be shunned by all, (695) as centres of
38 31 45   85   35 5   6   118   25

pestilence. (331) [1026]
182

All questions of the Law are to be decided only by
5   139   25 53   6   38 31 45   104   38 35

appeal to my writings, (782) each for himself. (178) [960]
81   31 36   115   43 37   98

There is no law beyond Do what thou wilt. [381]
90 28 21 6   87   13 32   52   52

Love is the law, (131) love under will. (148) [279] {4913}
44 28 53   6   44   74   30

The Facsimile of
Liber AL

Had! The manifestation of Nuit
The unveiling of the company of heaven
Every man and every woman is a star
Every number is infinite; there is no difference
Help me, o warrior lord of Thebes, in my unveiling before the children of men
Be thou Hadit, my secret centre, my heart & my tongue.
Behold! it is revealed by Aiwass the minister of Hoor-paar-kraat
The Khabs is in the Khu, not the Khu in the Khabs
Worship then the Khabs, and behold my light shed over you.

Let my servants be few & secret: they shall
rule the many & the known.

These are fools that men adore; both their
Gods & their men are fools.

Come forth, o children, under the stars
& take your fill of love. I am above you
and in you. My ecstasy is in yours. My
joy is to see your joy.

1. 1. If Spell called the Song.

Now ye shall know that the chosen
priest & apostle of infinite space is
the prince-priest the Beast; and in

his woman, called the Scarlet Woman, is
all power given. They shall gather my
children into their fold: they shall bring the
glory of the stars into the hearts of men.
For he is ever a sun, and she a moon. But
to him is the winged secret flame, and to
her the stooping starlight.
But ye are not so chosen.
Burn upon their brows, o splendrous serpent!
O azure-lidded woman, bend upon them!
The key of the rituals is in the secret word
which I have given unto him

With the God & the Adorer I am nothing: they do not see me. They are as upon the earth; I am Heaven, and there is no other God than me, and my lord Hadit.

Now therefore I am known to ye by my name Nuit, and to him by a secret name which I will give him when at last he knoweth me.

Since I am Infinite Space and the Infinite Stars thereof, do ye also thus. Bind nothing! Let there be no difference made among you between any one thing & any other thing other thing; for thereby there cometh hurt.

But whoso availeth in this, let him be
the chief of all!

I am Nuit and my word is six and fifty.
Divide, add, multiply and understand.
Then saith the prophet and slave of the
beauteous one: Who am I, and what shall
be the sign. So she answered him, bending
down, a lambent flame of blue, all-touching,
all penetrant, her lovely hands upon the
black earth, and her lithe body arched for love,
and her soft feet not hurting the

little flowers. Thou knowest! And the sky,

shall be my ecstasy, the consciousness of

the continuity of existence, the ~~matter~~ the

~~has atoms~~ omnipresence of my body, ~~part of~~

(~~Write this in other words~~) | One line as
                                    | above.

(~~But go further~~)

Then the priest murmured & said unto

the Queen of Space, kissing her lovely brow

and the dew of her light-laughing-holihide

body in a sweet-smelling perfume of Secret

6 Nuit, continuous one of Heaven, let it

be ever thus that men speak not of
thee as One but as None and let
them speak not of thee at all since
thou art continuous.

None, sheathed the light, faint of faery, of
the stars, and two for I am divided
for love's sake, for the chance of union.
This is the creation of the world that
the pain of ~~division~~ is as nothing and
the joy of dissolution all.
For these fools of men and their

...wes are not Thor at all! They feel little; what is, is balanced by weak joys: but spare my chosen ones.

Obey my prophet! follow out the ordeals of my knowledge! seek me only! Then the joys of my love will redeem ye from all pain. This is so: I swear it by the vault of my body; by my sacred heart and tongue; by all I can give, by all I desire of ye all.

Then the priest fell into a deep trance or

9

Soon I said unto the Queen of Heaven
Write unto us the ordeals write unto
us the rituals write unto us the law.
But she said the ordeals I write not
the rituals shall be half known and
half concealed: the law is for all
This that thou writest is the threefold
book of Law
My secret scribe Ankh-af-na-Khonsu the
priest of the princes shall not in one
letter change this book, but lest there
be folly, he shall comment thereupon
by the wisdom of Ra-Hoor-Khuit.

Also the mantras and spells; the
obeah and the wanga; the work of
the wand and the work of the
sword: these he shall learn and teach.
He must teach; but he may make severe
the ordeals.

The word of the Law is Θελημα.
Who calls us Thelemites will do no
wrong, if he look but close into the
word. For there are Three
Grades, the Hermit and the Lover and
the man of Earth. Do what thou wilt

shall be the whole of the Law.

The word of Sin is Restriction. O man!
refuse not thy wife if she will. O
lover, if thou wilt, depart. There is
no bond that can unite the divided but
love: all else is a curse. Accursèd!
Accursèd! be it to the aeons. Hell.
Let it be that state of manyhood
bound and loathing. So with my all
thou hast no right but to do thy will
Do that, and no other shall say nay
For pure will, unassuaged of purpose,

derived from the last of result, [12] is

every way perfect—

The Perfect and the Perfect are one

Perfect and not two; nay, are none!

Nothing is a secret key of this law

Sixty-one the laws call it; I call it

Eight, eighty, hundred & eighteen

But they halve the half... unto like

act so that all disappear.

My intellect is a fool with his one one

one: are not they the One and none

by the Book.

Abrogate all rituals, all ordeals, all
words and signs. Ra-Hoor Khuit hath
taken his seat in the East at the Equinox
of the Gods; and let Asar be with Isa
who also are one. But they are not of
me. Let Asar be the adorant, Isa the
sufferer; Hoor in his secret name and
splendour is the Lord initiating.
There is a word to say about the Hierophantic
task. Behold! There are three ordeals in
one, and it may be given in three ways.
The gross must pass through fire; let the

14

fine he there in intellect, and the

lofty more, ones in the highest. Thus

ye have there within system isgystin

let not one know well his other.

There are four gates to one palace,

The floor of that place is of silver and

gold, lapis lazuli _____ are there, and

all sweet scents jasmine & rose, and the

embles of death. Let him enter in then

or at once the four gates; let him stand

a the floor of the palace. Will he

not drink? Anon. Ho! warrior, if thy

servant drink? But there are _____

and mean   Be goodly therefore: dress ye
all in fine apparel eat rich foods and
drink sweet wine and wines That from.
~~but~~ Also, take your fill and will of
love as ye wish, when, where and with
whom ye will.   But always unto me
If this be not aught; if ye expound
the space-marks, saying: They are one
or saying They are many; if the ritual
be not unto me: the expect
the dreadful judgments of R. How What
This shall regenerate the world, the little

16

would my sister, my heart my tongue,
unto whom I send this kiss. Also, o
scribe and prophet though thou be of the
princes it shall not assuage thee nor
absolve thee. But restless be thine and
stir of earth. even To me To me

Change not as much as the style
of a letter; for behold thou o prophet
shalt not behold all these mysteries
hidden therein.
The child of thy bowels, he shall behold
them.
Expect him not from the East nor from

the West, for from no expected home
cometh that child. Ann! All words are
sacred and all, prophets true; save only that
, they understand a little; so we put
half of the equation, leave the second
unattributed. But thou hast all in the
clear light, and some thought not all in the
dark.

I woke me under my stars. Love is the
law, love under will. Nor let the fools
mistake love; for there are love and love.
There is the dove and there is the serpent.
Choose ye well! He, my prophet, hath

Chosen, knowing the law of the fortress
and the great mystery of the House of God.
All these old letters of my Book are
aright; but צ is not the Star. This
also is secret: my prophet shall reveal
it to the wise.

I give unimaginable joys on earth: certainty,
not faith, while in life, upon death; peace
unutterable, rest, ecstasy; nor do I demand
aught in sacrifice.

My incense is of resinous woods & gums;
and there is no blood therein: because of
my hair the trees of Eternity.

My number is 11, as all their numbers
who are of us. (*not?*) My colour is flesh. The
(*invoking me, the*) The Five Pointed star, with a
black, but the blue & gold are seen of the
circle in the middle, & the circle is Red
seeing. Also I have a secret glory for
them that love me.

But to love me is better than all things: if
under the night-stars in the desert thou
presently burnest mine incense before me,
invoking me with a pure heart, and the
Serpent flame therein, then shalt come
a little to lie in my bosom. For one kiss
wilt thou then be willing to give all.

but whoso gives one particle of dust
shall lose all in that hour. Ye shall
gather goods and store of women and
spices; ye shall wear rich jewels, ye
shall exceed the nations of the earth
in splendour & pride; but always in the
love of me, and so shall ye come to
my joy. I charge you earnestly to come
before me in a simple robe and crowned
with a birch headdress. . Ere you I grant to
you. Pale or purple, veiled or what you will,
who are old pleasure and purple

21

and unableheness / the un rerun / that
desire you.   Put on the wings and arouse
the coiled splendour within you : come unto me
At all my meetings with you shall be
priestess say – and her eyes shall burn
with desire as she stands bare and rejoicing
in my secret temple – To me! To me!
calling forth the hearts of all in her
love – chant.
Sing the raptures of love – say unto me!
Burn thine perfumes! Wear to me jewels!
Drink to me, for I love you! I love you!

and humbleness of the universe of that
desire you. Put on the wings and arouse
the coiled splendour within you: come unto me
At all my meltings with you shall be
sweetness say — and her eyes shall burn
with desire as she stands bare and rejoicing
in my secret temple — To me! To me!
calling forth the heart of all in her
love — chant.

... the raptures a love — say unto me!
Burn thou perfumes! Wear to me jewels!
Drink to me, for I love you! I love you!

I am the blue-lidded daughter of sunset, I am
the naked brilliance of the voluptuous night
sky

To me! To me!

The Manifestation of Nuit is at a
End.

1 Nu! the hiding of Hadit.

2 Come! all ye, and learn the secret that hath not yet been revealed. I, Hadit, am the complement of Nu my bride. I am not extended, and Khabs is the name of my House.

3 In the sphere I am everywhere the centre, as she, the circumference, is nowhere found.

4 Yet she shall be known & I never.

5 Behold! the rituals of the old time are black. Let the evil ones be cast away; let the good ones be purged by the prophet! Then shall this Knowledge go aright.

6. I am the flame that burns in every heart of man, and in the core of every star. I am

Life, and the giver of life; yet therefore is
the knowledge of me the knowledge of death.

7. I am the Magician and the Exorcist. I am the
axle of the wheel, and the cube in the circle.
"Come unto me" is a foolish word; for it is I that
go.

8. Who worshipped Heru-pa-kraath have
worshipped me; ill, for I am the worshipper.

9. Remember all ye that existence is pure joy;
that all the sorrows are but as shadows; they
pass & are done; but there is that which
remains.

10. O prophet! thou hast ill will to learn this
writing.

11. I see thee hate the hand & the pen; but I am

12 Because of me in Thee which thou knewest not-

13. for why? Because thou wast the knower, and me.

14. Now let there be a veiling of this shrine: now let the light devour men and eat them up with blindness.

15. For I am perfect, being Not; and my number is nine by the fools; but with the just I am Eight, and one in eight: Which is vital, for I am none indeed. The Empress and the King are not of me; for there is a further secret.

16 I am the Empress & the Hierophant. Thus eleven, as my bride is eleven.

17 Hear me, ye people of sighing!

   The sorrows of pain and regret
   Are left to the dead and the dying,

   The folk that not know me as yet.

18 These are dead, these fellows; they feel not. We are not for the poor and sad: the lords of the earth are our kinsfolk.

19 Is a God to live in a dog? No! but the highest are of us. They shall rejoice, our chosen: who sorroweth is not of us.

20 Beauty and strength, leaping laughter and delicious languor, force and fire, are of us.

21 We have nothing with the outcast and the unfit: let them die in their misery. For they feel not. Compassion is the vice of kings: stamp down the wretched & the weak: this is the law of the strong: this is our law and the joy of the world. Think not, o king, upon that lie: That Thou Must Die: verily thou shalt not die, but live! Now let it be understood If the body of the King dissolve, he shall remain in pure ecstasy for ever. Nuit! Hadit! Ra-Hoor-Khuit! The Sun, Strength & Sight, Light; these are for the servants of the Star & the Snake

6

22 I am the Snake that giveth Knowledge & Delight and bright glory, and stir the hearts of men with drunkenness. To worship me take wine and strange drugs whereof I will tell my prophet, & be drunk thereof! They shall not harm ye at all. It is a lie, this folly against self. The exposure of innocence is a lie. Be strong, o man, lust, enjoy all things of sense and rapture: fear not that any God shall deny thee for this.

23 I am alone: there is no God where I am.

24 Behold! these be grave mysteries; for there are also of my friends who be hermits. Now

Think not to find them in the forest or on the mountain; but in beds of purple, caressed by magnificent beasts of women with large limbs, and fire and light in their eyes, and masses of flaming hair about them; there shall ye find them. Ye shall see them at rule, at victorious armies, at all the joy; and there shall be in them a joy a million times greater than this. Beware lest any force another, King against King! Love one another with burning hearts; on the low men trample in the fierce lust of your pride in the day of your wrath.

25. Ye are against the people, O my chosen!

26. I am the secret Serpent coiled about to
spring: in my coiling there is joy. If I
lift up my head, I and my Nuit are one.
If I droop down mine head, and shoot
forth venom, then is rapture of the earth,
and I and the earth are one.

27. There is great danger in me; for who doth
not understand these runes shall make
a great miss. He shall fall down into
the pit called Because, and there he shall

down with the dogs of Reason.

28 Now a curse upon Because and his kin!

29 May Because be accursèd for ever!

30 If Will stops and cries Why, invoking
  Because, then Will stops & does nought.

31 If Power asks why, then is Power weakness.

32 Also reason is a lie; for there is a
  factor infinite & unknown; & all their
  words are skew-wise.

33 Enough of Because! Be he damned for a dog!

34 But ye, o my people, rise up & awake!

35 Let the rituals be rightly performed with
  joy & beauty!

36. There are rituals of the elements and feasts of the times.

37. A feast for the first night of the Prophet and his Bride!

38. A feast for the three days of the writing of the Book of the Law.

39. A feast for Tahuti and the child of the Prophet — secret, O Prophet!

40. A feast for the Supreme Ritual, and a feast for the Equinox of the Gods.

41. A feast for fire and a feast for water; a feast for life and a greater feast for death!

42 A feast every day in your hearts in the joy of my rapture.

43 A feast every night unto Nuit, and the pleasure of uttermost delight.

44 Aye! feast! rejoice! there is no dread hereafter. There is the dissolution, and eternal ecstasy in the kisses of Nu.

45 There is death for the dogs.

46 Dost thou fail? Art thou sorry? Is fear in thine heart?

47 Where I am these are not.

48 Pity not the fallen! I never knew them.
I am not for them. I console not: I hate
the consoled & the consoler.

49 I am unique & conqueror. I am not of the
slaves that perish. Be they damned &
dead! Amen. [This is of the 4: there is
a fifth who is invisible & therein am I
as a babe in an egg.]

50 Blue am I and gold in the light of my
bride: but the red gleam is in my eyes
& my spangles are purple & green.

51 Purple beyond purple: it is the light higher

than eyesight.

52 There is a veil: that veil is black. It is
the veil of the modest woman; it is the veil
of sorrow, & the pall of death. this is none
of me. Tear down that lying spectre of
the centuries: veil not your vices in
virtuous words; these vices are my service;
ye do well, & I will reward you here and
hereafter.

53 Fear not, o prophet, when these words are
said, thou shalt not be sorry. Thou art
emphatically my chosen; and blessed are

the eyes that thou shalt look upon with
gladness. But I will hide thee in a
mask of sorrow: they that see thee shall
fear thou art fallen: but I lift thee up

54 Nor shall they who cry aloud their folly
that thou meanest nought avail; thou
shalt reveal it: thou availest: they are
the slaves of because: They are not of
me. The stops as thou wilt; the letters
change them not in style or value!

55 Thou shalt obtain the order & value of
the English Alphabet; thou shalt find

new symbols to attribute them unto.

5⁵ Begone! ye mockers; even though ye laugh in my honour ye shall laugh not long: then when ye are sad know that I have forsaken you.

57. He that is righteous shall be righteous still; he that is filthy shall be filthy still.

58 Yea! deem not of change: ye shall be as ye are, & not other. Therefore the kings of the earth shall be Kings for ever: the slaves shall serve. There is none that shall be cast down or lifted up: all is ever

as it was. Yet there are marked men: my servants: it may be that yonder beggar is a King. A King may choose his garment as he will: there is no certain test: but a beggar cannot hide his poverty.

59 Beware therefore! Love all, lest perchance is a King concealed! Say you so? Fool! If he be a King, thou canst not hurt him.

60 Therefore strike hard & low, and to hell with them, master!

61 There is a light before thine eyes o prophet, a light undesired, most desirable.

62 I am uplifted in thine heart; and the kisses
of the stars rain hard upon thy body.

63 Thou art exhaust in the voluptuous fullness
of the inspiration; the expiration is sweeter
than death, more rapid and laughterful than
a caress of Hell's own worm.

64 Oh! thou art overcome: we are upon thee;
our delight is all over thee: hail! hail!
prophet of Nu! prophet of Had! prophet of
Ra-Hoor-Khu! Now rejoice! now come in
our splendour & rapture! Come in our passionate
peace, & write sweet words for the Kings!

65 I am the Master: thou art the Holy Chosen One.

66 Write, & find ecstasy in writing! Work, & be our bed in working! Thrill with the joy of life & death! Ah! thy death shall be lovely: whoso seeth it shall be glad. Thy death shall be the seal of the promise of our agelong love. Come! lift up thine heart & rejoice! We are one; we are none.

67 Hold! Hold! Bear up in thy rapture; fall not in swoon of the excellent kisses!

68 Harder! Hold up thyself! Lift thine head!

breathe not so deep — die!

69 Ah! Ah! What dost feel? Is the word
Exhausted?

70 There is help & hope in other spells. Wisdom
says: be strong! Then canst thou bear more
joy. Be not animal; refine thy rapture!
If thou drink, drink by the eight and ninety
rules of art: if thou love, exceed by
delicacy; and if thou do aught joyous, let
there be subtlety therein!

71 But exceed! exceed!

72 Strive ever to more! and if thou art

mine – and doubt it not; an if thou art
ever joyous! – death is the crown of all.

33 Ah! Ah! Death! Death! thou shalt long for
death. Death is forbidden, o man, unto thee.

74 The length of thy longing shall be the strength
of its glory. He that lives long & desires
death much is ever the King among the Kings.

75 Aye! listen to the numbers & the words:

76   4 6 3 8 A B K 2 4 A L G M O R 3 Y
     × 24 89 R P S T O V A L. What
     meaneth this, o prophet? Thou knowest
     not; nor shalt thou know ever. There
     cometh one to follow thee: he shall

Expound it. But remember, o chosen
one, to be me; to follow the love of
Nu in the star-lit heaven; to look forth
upon men, to tell them this glad word.

77 O be thou proud and mighty among men!

78 Lift up thyself! for there is none like unto
thee among men or among Gods! Lift up
thyself, o my prophet, thy stature shall
surpass the stars. They shall worship thy
name, foursquare, mystic, wonderful, the
number of the man; and the name of

thy house 418.

79 The end of the hunting of Hadit; and
blessing & worship to the prophet of
the lovely Star.

1 Abrahadabra! the reward of Ra Hoor Khut.

2 There is division hither homeward; there is a word not known. Spelling is defunct; all is not aught. Beware! Hold! Raise the spell of Ra-Hoor-Khuit!

3 Now let it be first understood that I am a god of War and of Vengeance. I shall deal hardly with them.

4 Choose ye an island!

5 Fortify it!

6 Dung it about with enginery of war!

7 I will give you a war-engine.

8 With it ye shall smite the peoples and

2

none shall stand before you.

9 Lurk! Withdraw! Upon them! This
is The Law of the Battle of Conquest: Thus
shall my worship be about my secret house.

10 Get the stélé of revealing itself; set it
in thy secret temple — and that temple
is already aright disposed — & it shall be your
Kiblah for ever. It shall not fade, but
miraculous colour shall come back to it
day after day. Close it in locked glass for a
proof to the world.

11 This shall be your only proof. I forbid argument.
Conquer! That is enough. I will make ea—

to you the abstraction from the ill-ordered house in the Victorious City. Thou shalt thyself convey it with worship, o prophet, though thou likest it not. Thou shalt have danger & trouble. Ra-Hoor-Khu is with thee. Worship me with fire & blood; worship me with swords & with spears. Let the woman be girt with a sword before me: let blood flow to my name. Trample down the Heathen; be upon them, o warrior, I will give you of their flesh to eat!

12 Sacrifice cattle, little and big: after a child.

13 But not now.

14 Ye shall see that hour, o blessèd Beast, and then the Scarlet Concubine of his desire!

15 Ye shall be sad thereof.

16 Been apt too eagerly to catch the promise; for not to undergo the curse. Ye, even ye, know not this meaning all.

17 Fear not at all; fear neither men, nor Fates nor gods, nor anything. Money fear not, nor laughter of the folk folly, nor any other power in heaven or upon the earth or under the earth. Nu is your refuge as Hadit your

light; and I am the strength, the peace, my ... of your arms.

18 Mercy let be off: damn them who pity. Kill and torture; spare not; be upon them.

19 That stele they shall call the Abomination of Desolation; count well its name, & it shall be to you as 718.

20 Why? Because of the fall of Because, that he is not there again.

21 Set up my image in the East: thou shalt buy thee an image which I will show thee, especially not unlike the one thou knowest. And it shall be suddenly easy for thee to do this.

6

22. The other images group around me to support
me: let all be worshipped, for they shall
cluster to exalt me. I am the visible object
of worship; the others are secret; for the Beast
& his Bride are they: and for the winners of
the Ordeal x . What is this? Thou shalt know.

23 For perfume mix meal & honey & thick leavings
of red wine: then oil of Abramelin and
olive oil, and afterward soften & smooth
down with rich fresh blood!

24 The best blood is of the moon, monthly: then
the fresh blood of a child, or dropping from the

host of heaven: then of enemies; then
of the priest or of the worshippers: last of
some beast, no matter what.

25 This burn: of this make cakes & eat unto
me. This hath also another use; let it be
laid before me, and kept thick with perfumes
of your orison: it shall become full of beetles
as it were and creeping things sacred unto me.

26 These slay, naming your enemies & they shall
fall before you.

27 Also these shall breed lust & power of lust in
you at the eating thereof.

28 Also ye shall be strong in war.

29 Moreover, be they long kept, it is better; for they swell with my force. All before me.

30 My altar is of open brass work: burn thereon in silver or gold.

31 There cometh a rich man from the West who shall pour his gold upon thee.

32 From gold forge steel:

33 Be ready to fly or to smite.

34 But your holy place shall be untouched throughout the centuries: though with fire and sword it be burnt down & shattered, yet an invisible house there standeth and shall stand until the fall of the Great—

Equinox, when Hrumachis shall arise and
the double-wanded one assume my throne and
place. Another prophet shall arise, and bring
fresh fever from the skies; another woman shall
wake the lust & worship of the Snake; another
soul of God and beast shall mingle in the
globed priest; another sacrifice shall stain
the tomb; another king shall reign; and blessing
no longer be poured To the Hawk-headed
mystical Lord !

35 The half of the word of Heru-ra-ha, called
Hoor-pa-kraat and Ra-Hoor-Khut.

36 Then said the prophet unto the God.

37 ladore thee in the song
"I am the Lord of Thebes" &c from Vellum book
——— "fill me

38 So that thy light is in me & its red flame
is as a sword in my hand to push thy
order. There is a secret door that I shall
make to establish thy way in all the quarters
(these are the adorations, as thou hast written)
as it is said.

"The light is mine" &c
from vellum book to "Ra - Hoor - Khuit

39 All this and a book to say how thou
didst come hither and a reproduction of
this ink and paper for ever — for in it is
the word secret & not only in the English —
and thy comment upon this the Book of the Law
shall be printed beautifully in red ink and
black upon beautiful paper made by hand;
and to each man and woman that thou
meetest, were it but to dine or to drink
at them, it is the Law to give. Then they
shall chance to abide in this bliss or no;
it is no odds. Do this quickly!

40 But the work of the comment? That is easy; and

Hadit burning in thy heart shall make swift and secure thy pen.

41. Establish at thy Kaaba ~~of~~ a clerk-house. all must be done well and with business way.

42. The ordeals thou shalt oversee thyself, save only the blind ones. Refuse none, but thou shalt know & destroy the traitors. I am Ra-Hoor-Khuit and I am powerful to protect my servant. Success is thy proof: argue not: convert not: talk not overmuch. Them that seek to entrap thee, to overthrow thee, them attack without pity or quarter & destroy them utterly. Swift as a trodden serpent turn

and strike! Be thou yet deadlier than he!

Bring down their souls to awful torment: laugh at their fear: spit upon them!

63 Let the Scarlet Woman beware! If pity and compassion and tenderness visit her heart; if she leave my work to toy with old sweetnesses; then shall my vengeance be known. I will slay me her child: I will alienate her heart: I will cast her out from men: as a shrinking and despised harlot shall she crawl through dusk wet streets, and die cold and an-hungered.

44. But let her raise herself in pride. Let her follow me in my way. Let her work the work of wickedness! Let her kill her heart! let her be loud and adulterous; let her be covered with jewels and rich garments. and let her be shameless before all men!

45 Then will I lift her to pinnacles of power. Then will I breed from her a child mightier than all the kings of the earth. I will fill her with joy: with my force shall she see + strike at the worship of Nu. she shall achieve Hadit.

46. I am the warrior Lord of the Forties: the
Eighties cower before me, & are abased.
I will bring you to victory & joy: I will be
at your arms in battle & ye shall
delight to slay. Success is your proof;
courage is your armour; go on, go on, in
my strength & ye shall turn not back for
any.

47. This book shall be translated into all
tongues: but always with the original in
the writing of the Beast; for in the

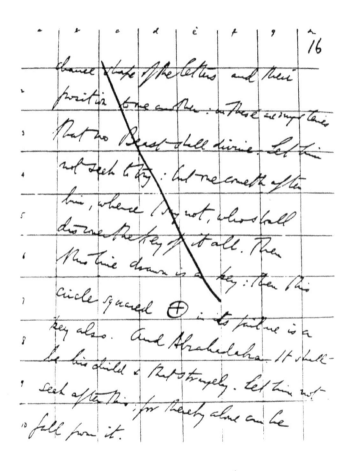

change shape of the letters and their
position to one another: in these are mysteries
that no Beast shall divine. Let them
not seek to try: but one cometh after
him, whence I say not, who shall
discover the key of it all. Then
this line drawn is a key: then this
circle squared ⊕ in its failure is a
key also. And Abrahadabra. It shall
seek after this: for thereby alone can he
fall from it.

48 Now this mystery of the letters is done, and
I want to go on to the holier place.

49 I am in a secret fourfold word, the blasphemy against
all gods of men.

50 Curse them! Curse them! Curse them!

51 With my Hawk's head I peck at the eyes of
Jesus as he hangs upon the cross

52 I flap my wings in the face of Mohammed &
blind him.

53 With my claws I tear out the flesh of the
Indian and the Buddhist, Mongol and
Din.

54 Bahlasti! Ompehda! I spit on your

crapulous creeds.

55 Let Mary inviolate be torn upon wheels: for her sake let all chaste women be utterly despised among you.

56 Also for beauty's sake and love!

57 Despise also all cowards. professional soldiers who dare not fight, but play: all fools despise

58 But the keen and the proud, the royal and the lofty: ye are brothers!

59 As brothers fight ye.

60 There is no law beyond Do what thou wilt.

61 There is an end of the word of the God

enthroned in Ra's seat, lightening the girders
of the soul.

62 To me do ye reverence; to me come ye
through tribulation of ordeal, which is
bliss

63 The fool readeth this Book of the Law, and
its comment & he understandeth it not.

64 Let him come through the first ordeal &
it will be to him as silver

65 Through the second, gold

66 Through the third, stones of precious water.

67 Through the fourth, ultimate sparks of the
intimate fire.

68 Yet to all it shall seem beautiful. Its
enemies who say not so, are mere liars.

69 There is success

70 I am the Hawk-Headed Lord of Silence
& of Strength; my nemyss shrouds the
night-blue sky.

71 Hail! ye twin warriors about the pillars of
the world! for your time is nigh at hand

72 I am the Lord of the Double Wand of Power
the wand of the ~~Force~~ Force of Coph Nia ~ I but my
left hand is empty, for I have crushed

an Universe & nought remains.

73 Paste the sheets from right to left and
from top to bottom: then behold!

74 There is a splendour in my name hidden
and glorious, as the sun of midnight is
ever the son

75 The ending of the words is the Word
Abrahadabra.

The Book of the Law is Written
and Concealed
Aum. Ha.

CPSIA information can be obtained
at www.ICGtesting.com
Printed in the USA
BVHW051813100222
628588BV00016B/539/J